Giovanna Magi

# PROVENCE

# INDEX

© Copyright by CASA EDITRICE BONECHI
Via Cairoli, 18/b Florence - Italy
Tel. +39 055576841 - Fax +39 0555000766
E-mail: bonechi@bonechi.it    Internet: www.bonechi.it

*Printed in Italy*
*by* Centro Stampa Editoriale Bonechi

*Photographs from the archives of Casa Editrice Bonechi
by* Luigi Di Giovine *and* Paolo Giambone.
*Page 20: photo by* Studio BERNATEAU, Orange
*Page 64, below: photos courtesy of the* "Château Musée de l'Empéri"
*Pages 68-74: photos courtesy of* PEC-Ph. Caudron

**ISBN 88-8029-324-9**

# INTRODUCTION

The problem that arises for people visiting Provence for the first time is which Provence to set out to see, to discover – in short, to admire – for spending too much time on only one of the region's facets means that you might lose sight of the others. This is why one trip to Provence is not enough: you need one trip to search out the Provence of the tiny villages perched upon craggy cliffs, another to discover the Provence of the gaily-coloured harbours with their fishing boats, another to take in the unconta- minated Provence of seem- ingly-endless Camargue horizons, gypsy pilgrim- ages, and herds of grazing cattle and horses, and still another to retrace the steps of the troubadours and the characters out of legend and history. And we must not forget the festivals held in the region which range from simple country fairs to sophisticated artistic and cultural spectacles that attract the intellectual elite of the whole world.

The language of Provence is still the dialect known as Oc, or Occitane, the tongue of the troubadours who sang of courtly love, requited and unrequited. It was in Merovingian times that Oc became different from the language spoken in the north of France known as Oil, and the difference has remained over the centuries.

Medieval Provence has left its special imprint: there are charming little abbeys half-hidden amidst the greenery and magnificent palaces once inhabited by popes. The country homes were called mas. They were huge buildings facing eastwards as defence against the mistral wind (master, in the local dialect) or the oustau when in built-up areas.

The presence of the mistral is only one of the ways that even nature is special in Provence. Indeed, there are many others: the red clay of Roussillon, the white limestone of Mont Ventoux, the notched Alpilles and

Lubéron chains, the barren garrigues (craggy limestone hills with sparse vegeta- tion), and the oak forests (now rare) and neat rows of cypress trees which offer respite from the raging mis- tral. And, too, the extensive fields of lavender, poppies, grapevines, and olive trees are proof of the love of the land deep-rooted in the Provençal population.

The people of Provence are strong and tradition-mind- ed. Even their way of speak- ing and gesturing reflects their long-ago heritage. Constantly they feel com- pelled to measure them- selves against the outside world.

In fact, this is symbolized by their favorite sport which is boules, a kind of bocce. Beneath the trees shading an improvised court, a pé- tanque player, his feet to- gether inside a circle drawn out on the ground, juggles the shiny metal ball as he prepares to make his play. Around him, the other play- ers and onlookers are already busily engaged in an animated discussion before the ball is even launched – but heated tempers will soon be cooled down by a sip of pastis.

Undeniably, over the last few decades, Provence, as every other place, has undergone a process of mod- ernisation and, of course, not everything is idyllic. Yet, in an era which has privileged the concept of civilisa- tion concentrated in just a few main centers around which exists nothing but vacuum, Provence is living proof of a more human and correct way of creating culture (in fact, this way of considering culture as part of a complex mosaic of activity is starting to come back again).

So, this is the problem – and challenge – for those who want to get to know Provence: they are faced with having to pick out the superimposed layers of civilisa- tions that, pieced together, explain the region's com- plex and fascinating historical truth.

# AVIGNON

The site where Avignon stands today has been occupied since earliest times. About two thousand years ago the Cavari peoples halted at a gigantic, rocky mass perpendicular to the Rhône and around this natural fortress they gave birth to an inhabited nucleus. These rough warriors and fishermen gave the name Aouenion to the city that they were developing, uniting the two Celtic words «aouen» which means a whirlpool, and «ion» which means lord, thus expressing in one word «lord of the waters.»

When, 600 years before the birth of Christ, the Phoenicians founded Massalia, that is Marseille, they were immediately attracted by the strong position of Aouenion and built a river port there which the Romans, in turn, did not fail to develop. Under their rule the name of the city became Avenio. In the history of Avignon there were not great events and, until the dawn of the 14th century, the city seemed destined to a mediocre, or at least anonymous future when, in 1309,

an event took place that was to fundamentally change its appearance and history: the Papal Court established itself at Avignon. Rome had become almost impossible for the popes to govern, exposed as they were to the struggles that rent the different competing factions. After the short pontificate of Benedict XI, who died in 1304, the Archbishop of Bordeaux, Bertrand de Got, was elected (helped by Philip the Fair, who wanted to make the Papacy an instrument of his will). He took the name Clement V and refused to go to Rome for the consecration which took place at Lyon instead.

Seeking a more worthy seat for the throne of Peter, John XXII, the successor of Clement V, installed himself at Avignon.

The period thus begun that passed into history as the «Avignon captivity» or «the Babylonian captivity of the Church,» from the title of the second reform writings of Martin Luther in 1520.

Seven French popes succeeded each other at Avignon

*The imposing mass of the Palace of the Popes at Avignon.*

*The Palace of the Popes seen from the river at night.*

and during this time the enormous papal fortress was built and fortified and the city was encircled by ramparts: the court at Avignon became one of the most splendid in medieval Europe.

But a strong movement of opinion was formed that desired the pope's return to Rome, his natural seat. Francis Petrarch, who was regularly at the Papal Court, was one of its most ardent supporters; Catherine of Siena long implored Gregory XI with sorrowful words («babbo mio dolce») (my sweet father) that he should leave the Provençal city; Brigetta of Sweden was another mouthpiece for the coming of an event that, by now, was desired by most of the Catholic world.

With Gregory XI, the transfer to Rome, in 1377, became definite even though with the election of an anti-Pope, the Christian world split and thus begun the Great Schism in the West.

Until the French Revolution Avignon was administered by a papal legate: during these truly happy years churches, monuments and hotels made the city more beautiful.

Only two great events troubled its existence: the first, the terrible plague of 1721 which left only one quarter of the population alive (it had been 24,000) the other was the unification of the city and the Venassin district with France in 1791.

## THE PALACE OF THE POPES

Built in about 30 years during the Pontificates of three popes (Benedict XII, Clement VI, and Innocent VI), this is one of the largest feudal castles: it consists, in fact, of a surface area of over 15,000 square metres. The exterior of the Palace of the Popes has the appearance of a true fortress with very high walls which are opened here and there by very narrow windows; powerful ogival arcades break up the mass of the building and huge machicolations made the castle almost invulnerable to any enemy attack.

Though the architects who saw to its construction were all French, the first, summoned by Benedict XII, was Master Pierre Poisson, he was followed by Jean de Louvres (who worked under Clement VI), the painters who were charged with the decorations were, on the other hand, all Italians: the Siennese Giovanni Luca and Matteo Giovannetti from Viterbo, who was called the «pittore del Papa» (the Pope's painter). The other Siennese Simone Martini worked in Avignon from 1339 to 1344 but not in the Palace of the Popes.

The entire architectural complex is made up of the union of two buildings: the so-called **Old Palace**, built by Benedict XII between 1334 and 1342, and the **New Palace**, built for Clement VI between 1342 and 1352. The last Pope completed the works. Unfortunately in the

*Palace of the Popes - The entrance to the palace and general view.*

course of the centuries the interiors have been altered. The years of the Revolution brought very serious damage: the furnishings were destroyed or scattered, and the statues and sculpture were burned. It was made into a barracks in 1810 and underwent a further disgrace, many of the frescoes were detached and sold to the antiquarians of Avignon, mutilated and in pieces.

From today, the fate of the Palace of the Popes will probably be very different. In 1969 the city decided to restore the two main wings of the palace and adapt them for use as a modern congress centre, leaving the exceptional beauty of the rooms perfectly intact, but giving it more modern fittings and more sophisticated equipment.

## THE HALL OF THE CONSISTORY

This enormous hall (34 metres long, 50 metres wide and 10 metres high) is one of the most important in the entire Papal Palace. In our day the Consistory no longer has the great importance that it had in the 14th century when it was the highest council and the high-

est court of the Christian world. Here, in this hall, with great pomp and ceremony, the pope summoned the cardinals. They entered through a small door in the south wall; sovereigns and ambassadors were received here; here the pope pronounced the names of those elected to the Sacred College; the process of canonizing Brigetta of Sweden was also undertaken here; it was here that Cola di Rienzo was judged and condemned (he was imprisoned for more than a year in the Tour de Trouillas).

We know that the walls of the hall, that have beautiful Gobelin tapestries today, were once covered by the frescoes of Matteo Giovannetti, but unfortunately the fire of 1413 that destroyed the entire wing of the Consistory did not spare the frescoes by the painter from Viterbo. Ever since the hall has been called the «salle brulée» (burnt hall) and that famous fire has left its sad mark in the typical rosy hue that is still on the stone of the east wall.

A door opens off a wall of the hall and leads to the **Chapel of St. John**, or the Chapel of the Consistory, which is covered by a pointed ribbed vault.

This, unlike the previous hall, has retained its wall

7

The Hall of the Consistory.

The frescoes in the Chapel of St. Martial and the Hall of Great Audience.

decoration, for the most part, intact. The north and the east walls are dedicated to the *life of St. John the Baptist* and the south and west walls to the *life of St. John the Evangelist.* In the vault is another large cycle of frescoes with figures of saints: these are so reminiscent of the style of Simone Martini, who was active in Avignon at exactly this time, that we would be tempted to attribute them to him. But in the list of accounts in the apostolic chamber no mention is made of the Siennese painter; on the contrary however there is recorded, in 1347, for this very chapel, Matteo Giovannetti from Viterbo, who worked here together with his team of artists between 1346 and 1348.

## CHAPEL OF ST. MARTIAL

This small chapel (it measures 6 metres by 5.25), situated on the first floor of the Tour St. Jean, owes its name to the fresco cycle by Matteo Giovannetti that depicts the *life of St. Martial,* the apostle and patron saint of Limoges and who, according to legend, was in fact a contemporary of Christ. The choice of the subject matter was without doubt determined by the fact that Pope Clement VI, under whom the Italian painter worked, was originally from Limoges. The scenes, which were painted between 1344 and 1345, begin in the vault. They then pass through the upper register

and on to the lower register of the walls, each scene is explained by a corresponding Latin inscription. All around the walls, below the two levels, runs a pediment of imitation marble supporting a Gothic arcade which is interrupted to make way for an *altar-piece* that many attribute to Matteo Giovannetti's own hand.

## HALL OF GREAT AUDIENCE

On the ground floor of the New Palace is the Hall of Great Audience, the masterpiece of Jean de Louvres. It is 52 metres long, 15.8 wide and 11 high, it was built in 1345 and is divided into two naves by a line of five composite columns which support the ribbing of the ogival arcade of the vault. The same ribbing rests on sculpted capitals that run along the wall, and are carved with representations of animals by anonymous artists, but are of a very high quality. In one of the vaults of the chamber, on a blue back-ground, studded with golden stars, the *twenty figures of the Prophets* and other Old Testament figures. They were done by Matteo Giovannetti in 1352-1353 for 600 gold florins. Each figure carries a phylactery (a parchment strip characteristic of the Jewish religion) bearing engraved maxims taken from their books. This chamber is also known as the «chamber of the major causes.» In the principal nave, which is partly separated from the rest

*The Room of the Deer and the fine painted tile pavement in the Pope's bedroom.*

of the room by a transenna, the 13 ecclesiastical judges who made up the Court of the «Sacra Romana Rota,» shortened more simply to Rota, would meet. The origin of this name is uncertain. It may be derived from the round bench for the 13 judges who were appointed by the pope and presided over by a dean (the «primus inter pares»); others believe it derived from the fact that each judge would try a case in turn, or else from the revolving lectern on which the manuscripts were placed. The birth of this court is very old: the earliest known regulations go back to 1331, under John XXII. Around the walled enclosure where the court was held lawyers who attended the cases and employees of the Papal Court grouped together. The remainder of the chamber was reserved for the public who made use of some benches set against the wall.

## THE POPE'S BEDROOM

Placed in the centre of the massive Tour de Pape, also called the «grand tower,» this is a square room, each side measuring about 10 metres with a corner fireplace and two windows. It is very possible that as soon as Clement VI had taken possession of this room he

*The frescoes in the Chapel of St. John.*

changed the wall decoration of his predecessor which was too stern and austere for his tastes. The walls are in fact covered with joyful and rich paintings composed of birds of many kinds that swoop among vines and squirrels that jump between the branches of oak trees. The whole is done in tempera and was painted directly onto the stone of the wall. Recently, using as a model the original tile floor that was discovered in 1963 in the «studium» of Benedict XII, the floor of this room has been covered with painted tiles, emulating those of the 14th century discovered during restoration of the Palace.

## THE ROOM OF THE DEER

This small, square room, situated on the third floor of the Tour de la Garde-Robe, has a much livelier and happier air compared to the other rooms that have come before it, due to the very special decoration that covers the walls. While all the previous rooms are decorated with sacred and religious subjects, this one has a secular subject which was very fashionable at that time; it shows the different kinds of hunting, from that using hawks to that employing dogs. It is the subject on the west wall that gave the room its name: here one sees an unleashed greyhound, pursuing, and about to bring down, a deer. Falconry is depicted on the east wall, with two figures, one of whom holds, in the traditional and customary manner, on the right finger, the bird of prey. On the north wall, however, is a fishing scene in which four figures are seen around a fish-breeding pond. This is certainly the «piscarium» which actually existed at the papal court of Avignon.

The frescoes were carried out in 1343 and are anonymous; it seems however that they were obviously inspired by Franco-Flemish tapestries which show subjects from the art of hunting and, exactly for this reason, they are attributed to the Frenchman, Robin de Romans, who was active in the court at this time. He was undoubtedly a painter of the second line among the large team of artists who worked for the pope. It is believed then that the subject matter, the elegance and the originality of the decoration must be French, but the experienced use of perspective and the plasticity of some of the figures are without doubt Italian. Due to this the supervision, or let us say the supervision of the works, should be attributed to Matteo Giovannetti who played a role of prime importance as the official painter of Clement VI.

# CATHEDRAL

The precise name of the cathedral at Avignon is **Notre-Dame-des-Doms**; perhaps this comes from the Latin form Domnus, a name given to ecclesiastical dignitaries; the church's name would then be Notre-Dame des Eveques (of the bishops) which in Latin is exactly de Domnis.

The origins of the church are vague: it may have been founded in the 4th century, it was rebuilt in Romanesque style and solemnly consecrated in 1069. The present building is still later, however, and dates from 1140-1160; during the centuries the Romanesque structure of the church underwent many changes. It was abandoned during the Revolution and was used again for worship in 1822. The history of the church is rich in events: in 1333, before leaving for the Crusades against the Turks, Philip VI of France, Philip of Navarre and John of Bohemia, received the cross which was to bless their «holy war» from Pope John XXII; in 1388 Clement VII was consecrated here in the presence of Charles VI, Louis II of Anjou, the King of Sicily and Jerusalem.

The entrance porch is inspired by Roman antiquity, with its fluted columns and Corinthian capitals; here Simone Martini, the Siennese painter who died in Avignon in 1344, painted the *Virgin surrounded by angels* and *Christ in the act of benediction* of which only sinopias are here today.

The interior is aisleless to which, between the 14th and the 16th century, the chapels were added. The apse was entirely rebuilt in the 17th century from a design by Louis François de la Valfenière. It contains five windows set into round arches. Here, what is thought to be the **tomb of Benedict XII** is kept; it is made up of many different pieces which have no relation to each other and which have been put together with the early and original tomb, erected in 1342-1345 by Jean Lavenier.

Another chapel contains the sepulchre of another pope, John XXII; due to the similarity of style and concept with bishops' tombs of the same period in the south of England, it has been suggested that it may have been done by the Englishman, Hug Wilfred. The *Bishop's chair is* also contained in the church. It is of white marble and dates from the end of the 12th century; on the sides are the symbols of the Evangelists Luke and Mark.

# CALVET MUSEUM

At no. 65 rue Joseph-Vernet stands the Hôtel Villeneuve-Martignan, built between 1741 and 1754. The building has a lovely wrought iron railing made in 1886 by Noël Biret of Avignon, which gives access to the courtyard of the palace.

Today this large and wealthy residence houses the col-

*The interior of Notre-Dame-des-Doms, the cathedral of Avignon.*

*The tomb of Benedict XII, inside the Cathedral.*

lections of the Calvet museums, named after its founder, Esprit Calvet; a professor in the faculty of Medicine in Avignon, an archeologist and a lover of books. At his death in 1810 he left to the city the enormous library, the art collections and the funds necessary to establish a museum. To this first nucleus other bequests and donations were added, such as the very important Greek marbles given by the Nani family of Venice.

**The stele of Rocher** – In the gardens of the Rocher des Doms, in 1960, a very important archeological discovery was made that was to overturn the theories that had been generally accepted concerning the origins of Avignon up to that moment. Until then, it was thought that the ancient tribes had settled and garrisoned this well-protected upland without ever giving birth to any form of civilization. The anthropomorphic stelae of curious manufacture and individual details have now shown that the early inhabitants of Avenio were not only more numerous, but also more advanced than had been thought up to that time.

## HÔTEL DES MONNAIES

In front of the Papal Palace stands the complex, baroque façade of the Hôtel des Monnaies, which today is a Conservatory of Music. It was built in 1619

for the papal legation of Cardinal Scipio Borghese whose coat-of-arms of dragons and eagles may be seen. The building later became a cavalry barracks and, during the years of the Revolution, the police headquarters. There is a marked contrast between the rather stark, almost military, appearance of the palace and the rich decoration of the façade.

## PETIT PALAIS

It is so called to contrast its small dimensions with those of the large «Palais» that stands nearby. The Petit Palais was built in 1317 and was laid out for Cardinal Arnaud de Via, nephew of John XXII. On his death it was bought by Benedict XII who made it the official residence of the bishop of Avignon. It was fortified during the Great Schism and was besieged and bombed. The palace received its present appearance during the second half of the 15th century; despite the fact that military and defensive parts were retained, the Renaissance architects were in fact able to introduce some elements more suited to the new taste: decorations and large rooms illuminated by windows that faced onto the river. Giuliano della Rovere, who was to become pope with the name Julius II, made it lovelier by important changes. In 1498 Cesare Borgia stayed here and in 1533, Francis I. When in 1663 Louis XIV passed through Avignon, Anne of Austria and the

*The façade of the Hôtel des Monnaies.*

*Petit Palais - The façade of the Palace and Botticelli's Madonna and Child in the Museum entrance.*

Duke of Orléans lodged there. When the state of Avignon was absorbed by France the palace was sold and in 1826 it became a seminary; in 1905 it was turned into a school for professional training and in 1958 it housed the Museum of the Middle Ages which united the Museum Calvet and the Campana collections.

From the many works of art a *Madonna and Child* stands out, in room XI; it is by Sandro Botticelli and is a small masterpiece from the Florentine painter's early period when he was able to impart to his Madonnas, which still reflected those of Lippi whose pupil he had been, easy linearity and a very delicate, almost languid state of mind.

14

## ST. PIERRE

This church, destroyed and reconstructed many times, was completely rebuilt in the 14th century at the expense of Cardinal Pietro da Prato, Bishop of Palestrina and Dean of the Sacred College. The church is exceptional for its façade, in splendid flamboyant Gothic style, from which, however, some early Renaissance elements are not absent; it was built in 1512 from plans by the painter-architect of Avignon, Philippe Garcin. In the centre of the façade is a majestic **entrance porch** with two carved *wooden doors* which no one would hestitate to put among the finest in the whole of Provence. These also were made possible by the generosity of a rich merchant of Spanish origin, Michel Lopis, who employed a carpenter of Avignon, Antoine Volard, born in Dauphiné; for a salary of 60 gold scudi he undertook to complete the doors. They were done in 1551 in solid walnut and are almost 4 meters high. The panels are sculpted in perspective and show, on the right, the *Annunciation,* and, on the left, *St. Michael and St. Jerome.* The impost above is decorated with bas reliefs and arabesques, figures of chimera, and angels supporting horns of plenty that overflow with flowers and fruit.

Inside, also, there are many works of art including a flamboyant Gothic *pulpit* and an *altar-frontal* in stone, made by Imbert Boachon in 1526.

## PLACE DE L'HORLOGE

The picturesque Place de l'Horloge is reached by way of the half-mile long Rue de la République which goes from the city walls of Avignon to the Palace of the Popes.

The present-day Place de l'Horloge, on the site of what was once the Roman *forum*, is now lined with cafés and coffeehouses which are favourite meeting-places for the young people of the whole area. On the square, in addition to the **theatre** is the **Hôtel de Ville**, an austere 19th century building. The Hôtel is built around the remains of the **Tour de l'Horloge**, all that is extant of a Gothic building, the Convent of the Dames de Saint-Laurent. The tower is also known as the Tour Jaquemart because it is surmounted by a carillon with two figures that strike the hours.

## ROCHER DES DOMS

The walls of Avignon, the famous Remparts, never cease to surprise all those who, having even a limited knowledge of military and defensive architecture, realize that this circle of walls is not a first-class work; whole sections of the machicolations are missing, there are open towers on the side of the city; what is lacking in fact is (for that age) a modern system of defence. But this, shall we say, lack of care in the wall fortification, happened because, in their Palace, the popes already had a fortress that was very difficult to

*Architectural detail of the portal of the church of St. Pierre.*

*The Place de l'Horloge.*

*The svelte arches of the Pont St. Bénézet.*

conquer. These Remparts were, so to speak, something extra, an addition that has become today an indispensable element in the traditional view of Avignon.

The walls were built between 1356 and 1370 and measure over 4 kilometres. They are elliptical in shape and have towers, turrets and, originally, seven gates that were later increased to 14. They were restored at the end of the 15th century by Cardinal della Rovere and restored a century later by Viollet-le-Duc. The **Rocher des Doms** makes a fitting reply to the walls of Avignon. It is the most characteristic place in the city and today is laid out as a garden. From here, like a sudden discovery, the majestic view of the Rhône opens out over the tower of Philip the Fair that stands on the other bank of the river, in Villeneuve.

## PONT ST. BÉNÉZET

This is the «pont d'Avignon» of the famous song that everyone knows. It is associated with a pretty legend, that of St. Bénézet who was never canonized but, it seems, actually existed.

The youthful Bénézet was still a young shepherd who watched over his flock in the vicinity of Viviers, where he was born, when, one day, he heard a heavenly voice that commanded him to go to Avignon and to build a bridge across the rushing course of the Rhône.

The boy, who had never before left his hills, met an angel on the way who led him to the Bishop of Avignon who tested him by making him lift up a rock that was so heavy that not even thirty men would be able to move it an inch. Bénézet, suddenly gifted with a miraculous strength, lifted it easily and took it and placed it on the bank of the river. «This rock will be» he said, «the first foundation of the bridge.» The crowd that had gathered behind in the meantime was gripped by an indescribable enthusiasm: there was immediately a public subscription which brought in, it is said, five thousand gold scudi.

Whatever the truth may be, be it legend or no, the building of the bridge began in 1177 and was completed in January 1185. It spanned the two arms of the Rhône and was about 900 metres long with 22 arches; to anyone, at that time, who sailed upriver from the sea this was the first bridge to be encountered. When Avignon fell in 1226 it was almost completely destroyed, it was reconstructed in part until it was definitely abandoned in 1680. All that remains today of the bridge are four arches with a small chapel on the second pier, made up of a Romanesque chapel surmounted by a Gothic chapel flanked by a 16th century apse. The body of Bénézet was buried here and in 1674 it was translated to the church of the Celestines but unfortunately this church disappeared during the stormy years of the French Revolution.

*Fort St. André, at Villeneuve-lès-Avignon.*

# VILLENEUVE-LÈS-AVIGNON

The medieval town of Villeneuve-lès-Avignon which stands on the right bank of the Rhône is almost the natural complement to Avignon. It was originally the Benedictine monastery of St. André which was founded in the 10th century on the hill that, in those times, was called Mont Andaon: at the beginning of the Middle Ages these heights were still an island, surrounded by one arm of the Rhône which, in time, dried up. In 1292 Philip the Fair, realizing the military and strategic importance of this site, began to build the new city, the «villeneuve» which was to counter-balance, as the mainstay of the Capetian monarchy, Avignon, the stronghold of the Empire, and later the city of the popes. The river simultaneously united and divided the two cities that confronted each other to such a degree that, after the campaign against the Albigenses, the King of France, who owned the river

but nothing else, wanted to tax the citizens of Avignon when, during the period of the floods, they were invaded by the waters of the Rhône that overflowed its banks. The arrival of the popes in Avignon was a golden opportunity for the new development of Villeneuve. The cardinals who were unable to find residences worthy of them in the papal city, moved into the «suburbs»: they crossed the bridge and built about 15 superb residences in Villeneuve, even after the popes had returned once again to Rome. Only the French Revolution put, forever, the word «end» to the aristocratic and ecclesiastic wealth that had typified life in Villeneuve for long centuries.

Many things remain from this splendid past. The first that, overbearingly, strikes the eye is the massive isolated **Tower of Philip the Fair**; built in 1302, at the beginning of the bridge of St. Bénézet; it is 32 metres

high and is all that remains of the little castle that originally defended the entrance to the bridge. During the 14th century a second floor and a small watch-tower were added. From the top there is a lovely view over the river towards the «city of the popes» that watches the «city of the cardinals.» There is another marvellous view from the top of the **Fort St-André.** This fortress was raised in the second half of the 14th century by John the Good and Charles V; it is completely enclosed by battlemented walls which are opened by a magnificent defensive entranceway, flanked by two powerful twin towers, dating from 1362; they were obviously inspired by northern military architecture and today they constitute one of the finest examples of medieval military fortification.

The opulent residence of Cardinal Arnaud de Via became a collegiate church in 1333. Today it is the parish church and has an imposing square apse made, in 1344-1355, of a tower crowned by battlements, and embellished by ogival, two-light windows. The interior, of a single nave, contains a small masterpiece kept in the sacristy: this, a many coloured **ivory Virgin**, carved from an elephant's tusk whose curve it follows in a sinuous and musical movement. This valuable little statue, a masterpiece of French 14th century sculpture, constitutes a necessary development from the seriousness and severity of the Gothic to the more manneristic style that was being born.

One of the most important monuments in the town is the **Certosa** (Chartreuse du Val de Bénédiction), built by Innocent VI to commemorate the gesture of the general of the Carthusian Order who, elected pope by the Conclave of 1352, refused the tiara out of humility and obedience to the Order. The Certosa, which in a short time became the most important in the whole of France, contains the Gothic **tomb of Innocent VI.** Made of stone it stands on a high pediment decorated with an arcade. There is also a small, very picturesque cloister; the cells of the monks face into a cloister, at whose centre there is a fountain named after St. John and there is also a courtyard with a well.

*The fine ivory figurine of the Virgin and Child, kept inside the Parish Church.*

*The Tower of Philip the Fair.*

*The Roman arch of Orange.*

# ORANGE

The ancient *Arausio* was born, primarily, as a Celtic settlement; it was actually here, in 105 B.C., that there was the first conflict between the Roman army and the Cimbri and the Teutons which was, however, a disaster for the former: 100,000 Romans were left on the battlefield. Arausio was founded by the veterans of the second legion of Julius Caesar and it enjoyed an enormous prosperity, particularly during the time of peace. All the great writers of antiquity mentioned it, from Titus Livy to Strabo, from Pomponius Mela to Pliny the Elder. Arausio, with four times its present population, had a theatre and an amphitheatre, baths and a circus, a triumphal arch (which

is in fact a commemorative arch) and many temples. Almost everything however was partly destroyed by the barbarians, the Alamanni and the Visigoths.
During the 13th century Orange was the seat of a small principality and, on account of that complicated game of marriages and inheritance with which history is replete, it fell to a branch of the Baux family who, at the same time, were heirs to the German principality of Nassau. When the famous William the Taciturn, who was prince of Orange and Nassau became governor of the United Provinces of the Low Countries, the name of this Provençal city became indissolubly bound to that of the then reigning dynasty in Holland. The

*The «frons scenae» of the theatre.*

Princes of Orange had such an interest in, and care for, their distant possession that they fortified it with a castle and a circle of walls. To do this however, they took the materials from the little that, centuries earlier, the barbarians had left standing. In this way, of the famous monuments in Orange, only the **triumphal arch** and the **theatre** remain.

Then, when Louis XIV went to war against Holland, the first to pay the cost was the principality of Orange: the walls were razed to the ground and the castle was destroyed. The Treaty of Utrecht of 1713 recognized France's possession of the principality.

Here we are at the few, but amazing, Roman monuments that have survived in Orange. Most important is the arch which was placed on the old via Agrippa that linked Arles and Lyon. It was built in 49 B.C. following a victory by Julius I Caesar and was reconsecrated to Tiberius in 25 A.D. 19 metres long, 18 high and 8 wide it is one of the most majestic that have survived. It has three openings and coffered vaults decorated with rosettes and surmounted by a tympanum and attic. The rich decoration commemorated the victories of the famous second legion who were the founders of the city. The war against the Gauls is celebrated on the upper level and alongside on the tympanum are two bas reliefs with subjects taken from the maritime world (anchors, prows and tridents); on one side there are prisoners in chains and war trophies.

The finest monument that antiquity has left us is the Theatre which was built under Augustus and is the only theatre in the world that still retains, absolutely and miraculously intact, the «frons scenae». It is imposing (103 metres long and 36 metres high), very elegant (it has openings on the lower level and is embellished higher up by blind arches); Louis XIV called it «the most beautiful wall of the kingdom.» The interior of the theatre originally had three levels and could hold 11,000 spectators. Today there are places for 7,000 who crowd in to every performance, thanks also to the perfect acoustics. In 1950 an enormous *statue of Augustus* was put back together and placed in a niche. This is one of the largest statues (it is 3,55 metres high) that was sculpted during the Imperial period.

Next to the theatre careful excavations by Formigé have brought to light the remains of an enormous **Gymnasium** that must have measured 400 metres by 80 metres.

It was probably made up of three running tracks, each 180 metres long, and surrounded by porticoes on two levels, of a platform on which wrestling matches took place, and this also had a colonnade around it. An imposing «**Capitol**» with three temples and a façade of 60 metres dominated the Gymnasium complex; it was strengthened by enormous buttresses that enclosed it at the sides. The excavations, carried out with care and attention, have revealed all this to us. If one climbs the St. Eutrope hill one realizes, from the remains of the temples and the arcades, the brilliance and complexity of the buildings.

*The interior of the theatre with the statue of Augustus.*

*A view of the excavations of the Gymnasium complex and the «Capitol».*

# VAISON-LA-ROMAINE

Without this town, laid out on the banks of the Ouvèze, a trip among the beauties of Roman Provence would not be complete. This place was already inhabited by a Neolithic people in the second millennium before Christ; in fact, beneath the Roman pavements traces of this period have been found, these consisted of stone hatchets and flint weapons and utensils. At the end of the 4th century B.C., at the time of the Celtic expansion, the city became the capital of a Celtic tribe, the Voconzi. The city was then to become «Vasio Vocontiorum.» The river, today the Ouvèze but in ancient times the Ouas, was to give its name to the city, that came to be called Ouas Jon, that is the city of the Ouvèze, which then became Vasio and finally Vaison. The military campaign under the Roman Consul M. Fulvius Flaccus in 124 B.C. marked its conquest which was confirmed with the peace of 58 B.C. and Julius Caesar bestowed on it the title of «civitas foederata»; that is a city allied with the people of Rome with all the political, economic and administrative advantages that this privileged position brought.

The importance and wealth of the city increased so much that the Roman historian Pomponius Mela called it the «urbs opulentissima.» It was exactly this opulence that marked Vaison's destiny, whetting the appetite of the different barbarian tribes that overran the area. The Ostrogoths, the Visigoths and the Burgundians put an abrupt end to Vaison's time of prosperity and destroyed it. As a result of this the population left the early site on the river and moved higher up, to the safety of the castle built on a precipitous rocky outcrop above the river. In the 18th century however the majority of the inhabitants returned to the site of the Roman city thus giving birth to and developing the modern town.

The archeological excavations, begun in 1907, have brought to light the enormous area of the Roman city which was divided into two districts: that of Puymin and that of Villasse.

In the latter, by following the main street which is a wide, paved road in whose pavement there are several holes for drainage, one reaches the large **Basilica**; for the ancient inhabitants of Vaison this was the business and commercial centre. All that remains of this today is a spacious hall, 12 metres by 50 metres, and a large arch supported by fluted piers.

In the district of Puymin another curious witness to the public life that was led at Vaison may be found: a *dolium,* an enormous wineskin for provisions, 2.2 metres high; this has been put back exactly in its original place, that is in the corner of a building complex that today we would not hesitate to call apartment blocks.Nearby is the **Portico of Pompey.** It was built perhaps, as is suggested by a fragment of inscription which carries the name Pompeia, thanks to the generosity of a member of this noble Roman family.

This place must have been a lovely and elegant public meeting place. It is square in form, each side is 52 metres long, with a large central area that is laid out as a garden today. The decoration must have been very fine with mosaics and frescoes on the walls and statues in the niches. On the north wall, in a semi-cirular exedra, is the *statue of the Empress Sabina,* the wife of Hadrian. The *statue of Hadrian is* in the eastern exedra; both these statues are copies of the originals in the Museum of Vaison.

In another niche is the Roman copy in white marble of the famous *Diadumenos*, a work by the great Polycletus, which is kept in the British Museum in London.

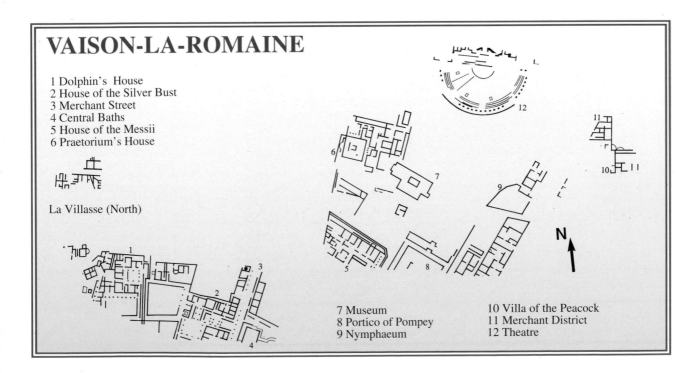

# VAISON-LA-ROMAINE

1 Dolphin's House
2 House of the Silver Bust
3 Merchant Street
4 Central Baths
5 House of the Messii
6 Praetorium's House

La Villasse (North)

7 Museum
8 Portico of Pompey
9 Nymphaeum
10 Villa of the Peacock
11 Merchant District
12 Theatre

*The Pretorium building.*

*A view of the House of the Messii.*

From here it is easy to get to the **Theatre** which is a little smaller than the ones in Arles and Orange and, like that at Orange it is set against a hill, the Puymin. It was built in Christian times and was in use until the beginning of the 5th century when, in 407, a decree by Honorius ordered the destruction of everything that could be asssociated with paganism. Material was then taken from it and used for the construction of new buildings. The stage is completely hollowed out of the rock of the hill; a tunnel was in fact carved out of the hill in order to give those who lived on the upper slopes access to the theatre. Despite the destruction, the upper level of the portico's colonnade still exists, in contrast to the other ancient Provençal theatres.

## THÉO DESPLANS ARCHEOLOGICAL MUSEUM

The Museum, housed in a building inside the area of Puymin, has on exhibit most of the finds which came to light in the excavations of past years.
The rooms are arranged around a large central hall, which also contains the sales desk for publications regarding the excavations of Vaison-la-Romaine.

*Tragic mask, from the acroterium of the mausoleum.*

*View of the theatre, set against the hill of Puymin: the tiers were originally decorated with statues of Hadrian, his wife Sabina and the Diadumenos.*

Mosaic from the villa of the Peacock and statue of Claudius, who was emperor from 41 to 54.

Head of Apollo crowned with laurel: for a long time it was thought to be a head of Venus and it was found in the house of the Messii in 1925.

Silver bust of a Roman patrician (second half of the 2nd century A.D.), found in 1924 in the quarter of Villasse among the ruins of the peristyle of a Roman house.

*Two views of the basilica.*

*Cathedral of Notre-Dame - The exterior of the church, in Provençal Romanesque, and, below, the nave.*

*Cathedral of Notre-Dame - a view of the cloister and a detail of one of the capitals.*

*The fine Roman bridge spanning the river Ouvèze.*

## CATHEDRAL OF NOTRE-DAME

The Cathedral of Notre-Dame was first built during the Merovingian period (6th or the 7th century) and was then rebuilt in Provençal Romanesque style between 1150 and 1160, using materials that came from different Roman monuments. Thus one can see that the *foundations* of this sacred building rest directly on Roman capitals and drums of Roman columns. The same method was used in the choir where the blind arcades rest on Roman columns intentionally placed there. Heavily restored, but going back to the middle of the 12th century, is the **cloister**. It is set against the north side of the cathedral. Its arcades are made up of small twin columns with decorated capitals and entwined leaves. Here there is a strange and long inscription in Latin; it is a half allegorical, half mystical text that has not yet ceased to cause historians and specialists in epigraphs to ponder.

## THE BRIDGE

The bridge over the Ouvèze still exists exactly as it was two thousand years ago; only the parapet was reconstructed during the last century after it had been destroyed by a flood in 1616. Once more destroyed by the flood of 1992, the parapet was rebuilt in 1994 in its original form. It consists of a single round arch which is very high above the river bed, and is 17 metres long. The later centuries at Vaison-La-Romaine have also left lovely remains.

*The castle which dominates the village of Le Barroux.*

*The abbey of Sainte-Madeleine, which stands in the midst of olive trees, cypresses and orderly lavender bushes.*

# LE BARROUX

The **castle** that was built by the lords of Baux on the top of the hill which dominates the village of Le Barroux looks like a real inexpugnabile fortress. As the centuries passed, the castle was transformed into a more pleasant Renaissance château, above all after the Barroux. The story of the **Abbey of Sainte-Madeleine** is, however, much closer in time. On August 25, 1970, Dom Gérard, founded the monastery of Sainte-Madeleine in Bédoin, in the department of Vaucluse. In but a few years the monastic community had grown to such an extent that in January of 1977 it was decided to build a larger monastery. The following year 30 hectares of land were bought from the town of Le Barroux. Work proceeded swiftly, even if not always smoothly, and on March 21, 1980, the first stone was laid, engraved with the motto of the monastery «Pax in lumine». The following year, at Christmas, the monks left Bédoin and moved to the new monastery. A church was soon added to this initial structure. Begun in January of 1986, construction lasted not much over three years. On June 18, 1989 the title of Benedectine Abbey was conferred on the monastery of Sainte-Madeleine.

# MONT VENTOUX

Mont Ventoux, 1912 metres high, is one of the most delightful sights in the whole of Provence. From the top there is one of the most majestic panoramas that can be enjoyed by the human eye: Marseille, the sea, the Alps, the Cevenne and the Pyrenees.

Curiously enough the ancient writers, particularly Pliny and Strabo, make no mention of this mountain. Also the first man in history to climb it, officially, was not, so to say, a professional climber but rather a poet: Francis Petrarch.

On the 26th April 1336, together with his brother, he set out from the village of Malaucène making his way towards the slopes that led to the summit. This ascent is commemorated today by a memorial stone set into the façade of the important weather station that has been built at the top.

In the 15th century a chapel dedicated to the Holy Cross was erected there. Here the Bishop of Carpentral, Pierre de Valetariis, placed a fragment of the True Cross into the care of a hermit; the chapel later became a place of pilgrimage. Mont Ventoux has always attracted the attention and the curiousity of botanists. The most varied kinds of flowers and trees are found here, from Mediterranean thyme to saxifrage from the Spitzberg! Also pine, cedar, fir and beech... At the summit the mistral blows with extreme violence: the mountain's name also testifies to this. During the winter the thermometer goes down to $-27°$ and, between December and April, above 1300 metres, the mountain clothes itself in white. Here also folk belief has tried to give a mysterious and supernatural explanation for the fury of the wind that unleashes itself here as in no other place.

During the diggings for the construction of the observatory many pieces of potsherds came to light; they seemed to belong to terracotta trumpets. The conclusion was drawn that this was a repository for votive offerings in a temple that, once, must have stood exactly here; a temple dedicated to the god of the place. The many shepherds of the area must have come here and left, with rituals, these trumpets into which they blew as offerings to the «wind-god.»

*Panorama on the top of Mont Ventoux.*

The neoclassic façade of the Hôtel-Dieu.

The lively picturesque city centre.

# CARPENTRAS

Bathed by the waters of the Auzon and dominated by Mont Ventoux, Carpentras was the indisputed capital of the powerful Venaissin county from the 2nd April 1320 to the Revolution, and was directly owned by the Holy See.

Pliny mentions it by the name of «Carpentoracte Menimorum» as capital of the Memini Celts. As for the name Carpentoracte, it would appear that it comes from the Celtic word «karpenton», meaning a horse-driven two-wheeled cart. It then became *Forum Neronis* and was the site of a flourishing market in Roman times. Carpentras developed rapidly. Shortly, it sprawled beyond its walls, which was why fortifications were doubled during the 14th century; all that remains of the second enclosure which included 32 towers and 4 gates is the **Gate of Orange**, providing access to the town. Carpentras also boasted one of the largest, liveliest Jewish communities in France; its synagogue is the oldest (1307) and best preserved in France. This is also proven by the magnificent Jewish door of **St. Siffrein Cathedral**, thus named because converted Jews were baptized there.

This portal is crowned by an unusual sculpture, whose meaning is still not quite clear: a ball with running rats on top; it is therefore named «boule aux rats» (rat ball). If we recall that the black plague, which was brought to Europe from the East by these rodents, killed over 150,000 people in Avignon alone and that in Carpentras three thousand died within the space of three years, it is a logical deduction that this sculpture served as a souvenir and exorcist of an unforgettable event.

The Cathedral itself was built in 1404 by Benedict XIII, the last antipope of Avignon, and it also contains the sarcophagus of Cardinal Butti by the Provençal artist Jacques Bernus, who also decorated the choir. Among the numerous other buildings in Carpentras, mention must be made of the **Hôtel-Dieu**, founded by Bishop Malachia of Ingiumbert, with its beautiful Neoclassic façade, whose columns support the triangular pediment crowned by a balustrade. Inside, one can admire an interesting pharmacy, whose painted cupboards contain a valuable collection of Moustiers ceramics.

# L'ISLE-SUR-LA-SORGUE

In olden times this place where one of the most typical Provençal towns is now to be found was a vast un-healthy swampy zone. A few families of fishermen settled here and, to improve living conditions, drained and reclaimed these lands, which were called «insu-lae». For a long time they enjoyed various privileges, first among which was the exclusive right to fish in the waters of the Sorgue, from its source up to the Rhône.

As time passed, this nucleus - which originally was called Saint-Laurent - was fortified so it could be defended from the attacks of the armed bands which roamed the area and plundered the neighboring villages.

Nothing remains of the city walls which were enlarged and renewed more than once in the course of the centuries, for they were completely torn down in the course of the 19th century.

We know however that there were four city gates of which one, known as Saint-Louis, had a fine pediment decorated with the coat of arms of the kings of France. Almost magically settled along the various arms of the river which crosses and cuts it with numerous canals, connected by small bridges and walkways which lead to the houses, the Isle-sur-la-Sorgue has a charm all its own. It has often been compared to Venice, and is

*The canals which run through the town.*

*Four pictures of the typical shops to be found in the centre of L'Isle-sur-la-Sorgue.*

*Exterior and interior of the Collegiate Church of Notre-Dame-des-Anges.*

even called the «peasant Venice», and the great plane trees which shade the boulevards, the heavy paddle water wheels, covered with dripping green moss make proud show. The water wheels were once used to to turn mills and presses and spinneries, and bear witness to the importance of these industries in the past. This quiet beauty is unexpectedly animated every Sunday when the streets along the canals fill up with booths and second-hand dealers. It might be said that L'Isle-sur-la-Sorgue has become the capital of the antique trade in the region, thanks also to one of the most famous antique fairs held there every year on August 15th.

Leaving the quietly flowing water of the canals behind us, we move into the streets of L'Isle-sur-la-Sorgue: here shops of Provençal crafts alternate with antique shops, boutiques selling the elaborate costumes typical of the region are set next to stores which sell lavender and honey, soap and essential oils. Passing from one perfume to the other, from a more delicate fragrance to a more intense and persistent one.

The most important building in the town is without doubt the **Collegiate Church of Notre-Dame-des-Anges**, a true gem of Provençal Baroque art. It was first built in 1222, by the bishop of Cavaillon, but was altered and rebuilt more than once in the course of the centuries, and the building we see today is in its 17th century form.

The contrast between the classical façade and the sumptuous Baroque interior could not be greater. The single nave divided into six bays is the work of the architect François de Royes de la Valfenière. The sumptuous glory in gilded wood and the high altar with its baldachin in polychrome marble are also particularly beautiful. L'Isle-sur-la-Sorgue still has other treasures in wait: the massive **Tour d'Argent**, known also as Tour Boutin, of medieval times, square in plan built on the Market Square, the **Chapel of the White Penitents**, of 1562, and the **Chapel of the Blue Penitents**, three years later; and then the **Ursuline Chapel**, of the end of the 16th century and that of the **Congregation of the Men** of the 17th century.

# FONTAINE DE VAUCLUSE

What kind of people go to Vaucluse, one of the most famous places of interest in the south of France? Above all those who love to retreat into solitary and beautiful places; lovers of poetry go there to seek the spirit of Petrarch and the echo of his love poems for Laura among the old walls of the castle; enthusiasts of the phenomena of water, because here, at the spring of Sorgue, there is one of nature's liveliest spectacles.

But let us begin at the beginning. The origins of this small settlement are linked to the name St. Véran. He was the Archbishop of Cavaillon around the middle of the 6th century, and according to legend he freed the region from a monster, an enormous reptile called Coulobre. A priory was situated here at the end of the 10th century, donated in 1034 to the abbey of St. Victor in Marseilles. For a long time the city and the castle, which is today in ruins, came under the sway of the Bishops of Cavaillon.

Francis Petrarch lived here for longer or shorter periods between 1337 and 1353 as the guest of his friend Philippe de Cabasso, the Bishop of Cavaillon. Here he conceived his most important Latin works, and it was here that he sang of his ideal and eternal love for

*The Sorgue at Fontaine de Vaucluse.*

*The column erected to Francis Petrarch on the occasion of the fifth centennial of his birth.*

The castle which dominates Fontaine de Vaucluse was the residence of Philippe de Cabassale, a friend of Petrarch's and bishop of Cavaillon.

The façade of the small church of St. Véran.

Petrarch Museum - Founded in 1927, this museum is situated on the left bank of the Sorgue in what seems to correspond more or less to the house where Petrarch once lived.

Laura, a love that was to fill the whole of the poet's life, a love which, as he himself wrote, kept him «anni vent'uno ardendo» («aflame for twenty one years.») Petrarch tells of how he met Laura de Noves, the wife of Hugues de Sade to whom she bore 11 children, for the first time on the 6th of April 1327, in the church of St. Claire in Avignon; on the same date, the 6th April, twenty one years later, by a strange and poetic coincidence, Laura died, struck by the terrible Black Death of 1348. A **column** was set up in Petrarch's honour in 1804 to mark the fifth centenary of his birth. However the best mementoes of the poet are found in the little **museum** laid out in a building which is said to have been constructed on the very site of the house in which the poet lived. It's not true then, that Petrarch stayed in the **castle**, which is now completely in ruins, and the ancient property of the Bishops of Cavaillon. Clinging to a high rock, the old manor-house dominates the countryside beneath and the rocks through which the foaming water of the Sorgue surges. The main sights for visitors to Vaucluse are the museum, the column and the castle, together with the little village church. The **Church of St. Véran** is a small, Romanesque building of the 11th century, it has no aisles, the transept is covered by a roof and the semicircular apse has a half-domed vault. On either side of it there are ancient, marble columns with Roman capitals. But, for once, more than the monuments and works of art of Fontaine de Vaucluse, it is nature that is the monument, and why not, the work of art. Walking in the steps of the great poet, who sought inspiration in solitude for his best verses, suddenly the **Sorgue spring** appears, here finally are the «chiare, fresche, e dolci acque» («the clear, fresh and sweet waters»). Quite apart from the majestic, picturesque scenery, full of charm which unexpectedly reveals itself, the Sorgue spring is also one of the richest and most abundant in

*THE PAPER MILL*

*The cultural and craft centre «Vallis Clausa» was created in 1974 with the principal aim of recreating the setting of an old paper- making mill. The paper industry was particularly important here in Fontaine: all of six mills employed as many as 450 workers. Today we can follow the ancient procedure, beginning with the great water-wheel with 48 paddles, two metres wide and seven metres in diameter, which moves a camshaft six metres long; revolving around itself the camshaft raises one after the other fifteen firwood mallets, each weighing 75 kilos and reinforced by sharp nails. These mallets are lowered and raised over five granite tubs filled with water, shredding the old rags in them, which, after being worked from between 24 to 36 hours, have turned into a white paste. At this point, the man in charge of the mixing uses a wooden frame over which a metal net is stretched to extract the amount of paste required for a sheet, shakes the frame slightly and lets the paste drip for a moment, then lays the sheet on a wool felt mat, in alternating layers until there is a pile of 100 sheets and 101 felt mats. This pile is then pressed and loses from 40 to 60 percent of the water. At this point the only thing left to do is dry the leaves, which are hung on racks where they continue to lose their humidity and wrinkle even more.*

the world. Its source may be the outlet of an immense underground river that is fed by the rain water and the water that drains from the uplands of Vaucluse, from Mont Ventoux, Luberon and the Lure mountains. As yet, it has been impossible to determine the course of this underground river which is the real nucleus which joins together the different tributaries of an immense water network; this despite many attempts, both in the past, such as that of Ottonelli of Marseille in 1869, and more recent ones, such as that of Commander Cousteau. At the bottom of a natural hemicycle of precipitous rocks is the cave from which the water of the Sorgue bursts. When the jet of the spring is more than 22 cubic metres per second a lively scene may be witnessed as the water, which takes on a very intense green tone, bursts from its usual pool and throws itself with great force over the surrounding rocks. At certain times of year, usually between Easter and Pentecost, the jet of water at its peak can reach 200 cubic metres per second, thus creating a truly impressive sight. Fontaine de Vaucluse also has something else of interest which is bound up with a legend. The left bank of the spring is dominated by a hill, vaguely in the shape of a cow's head and is, in fact, called «Vache d'or.» But why «of gold»? According to tradition an inestimable treasure in huge gold lingots is hidden inside this hill and is closely watched over by a spirit-guardian. If anyone tries to gain possession of this wealth the guardian lets out bellows, and then other loud menacing yells that rebound and re-echo from the depths of the mountain.

The icy waters of the Sorgue spring, just after leaving its source, do not stop the more daring from diving into the water.

On this page the two pictures, above, and below, left, were taken from the same position, but at different times of the year. In the first the spring is full of water and the cavity is completely submerged. In the second, taken in summer, the cavity is completely uncovered, and it is easy to go into the water. At the side: the waters of the Sorgue overflow and become an impetuous river.

*The fine Renaissance forms of the Château of Gordes and a panorama of the village.*

# GORDES

The village of Gordes is built on a rocky crag over-looking Coulon plain; its stone houses are huddled together in higgledy-piggledy fashion. The need for defence against invasions and enemy attacks during the Dark Ages meant that the majority of villages were built on top of hills. Nowadays walking around Gordes means discovering picturesque corners, sudden glimpses and unusual perspectives. A breathtaking view can be beheld from the **Castle**, built by Bertrand de Simiane on the site of a pre-existing Medieval fortress of the 12th century. Only two towers of the original nucleus are still standing; its present Renaissance shape dates back to the first half of the 16th century. The northern façade is distinguished by two spectacular round towers crowned by machicolations, with a tower above, while the opposite façade is opened by three storeys of windows. A large hall 23 metres long and with a wooden ceiling on the first floor features a huge fireplace, sculptured in 1541 with ancient motifs and crowned by thirteen niches, whose statues have since been removed.

It is worth mentioning that five halls in the Castle house the interesting **Vasarély Museum**, opened in 1970.

*The Château, with the old entrance doorway in the court, a typical street and a characteristic building in the «Bories» village.*

# «BORIES» VILLAGE

The «Bories» village or «black village» is situated a couple of kilometres from Gordes on the slopes of the Luberon. The «bories» themselves are huts of dried stones on one or more floors; they vary in shape and are built separately or grouped together in characteristic complexes. The word «bories» comes from the Latin «boaria», meaning cowsheds and, transformed into Provençal, it has come to mean type of country house. This concentration in Gordes is the highest in France; in fact, about three thousand huts have been catalogued. But where did they come from?

Even if the ones that are still standing were inhabited only as far back as the 16th century, it is an indisputable fact that their building system dates back to the Neolithic Age. On the other hand, how can one not find close analogies with other buildings in the Mediterranean area such as the Sardinian nuraghe or Greek tholos. How can one not think of the dome vault of the so-called «Tomb of Agamemnon» or Treasure of the Atridae in Mycenae? The majority of these huts were used as pig-sties or tool-sheds; only the small minority were used as homes. In the «black village» of Gordes, the huts are grouped around a central space, which was used for village activities. They are built directly on the ground without foundations; the walls are thick and feature only door and window openings. Inside the lived-in huts, the floors were tiled and the second floor was used as the sleeping area. As for furniture, it was reduced to a bare minimum: a fireplace, table, some chairs and household objects.

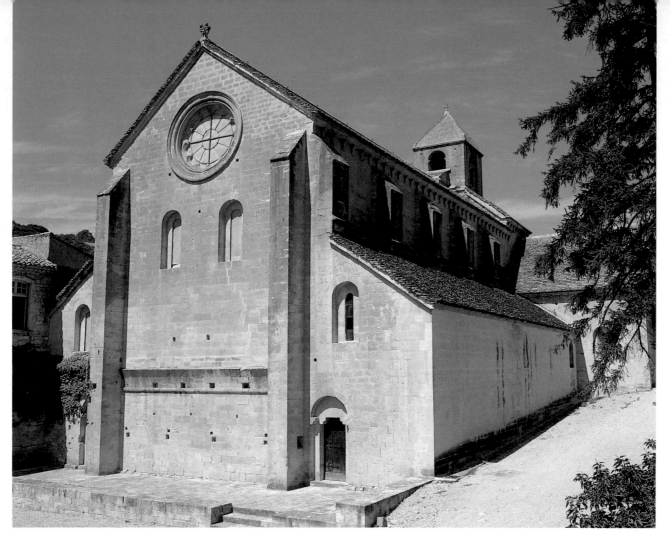

*A view of the «Bories» village, a detail of a bakery and an ancient almond tree that has grown inside.*

*On this and the following pages, a few views of the Abbey of Sénanque.*

# SÉNANQUE ABBEY

Founded at the end of the 11th century, the Cistercian order had already enlightened Western Christendom. When, in 1112, Bernard de Clairvaux came to the fore, the new monastic order reached the height of its glory. Faithful to one of Bernard's basic rules, which ordered the building of abbeys in isolated places far from worldly temptations, Sénanque Abbey (the last of the «three Provençal sisters», together with Le Thoronet and Silvacane) rose in an isolated valley, surrounded by the green of the forest. It was founded in 1148 by monks from Mazan under the direction and guidance of Peter, the first abbot of Sénanque: he then remained there for 34 years. The abbey was active until the outbreak of the religious wars, which dealt a cruel blow to life in the monastery; in fact, they set fire to it in 1544. Having miraculously escaped the revolutionary tempest, it was restored and flourished. Nowadays the monks are back in the Abbey where they live a con-

templative life according to Cistercian tradition. The stark beauty of the surrounding countryside enhances the solemnity and elegance typical of Cistercian architecture: the interior of the church is in the shape of a Latin cross with three naves, five apses and an octagonal dome at the crossing of the transept; the chapter house, with the ribs of the vault starting from the central bundle pillars; the magnificent cloister with its Provençal style arcades around the little garden, dominated by the square bell-tower and the monks' dormitories, with their huge, austere barrel vaults. In this environment, the Cistercian monks led a life of work and prayer; their days were broken up by the holy offices, which were carried out in the greatest simplicity. It was thanks to this sense of brotherhood and spirituality that the abbeys flourished; on Bernard's death, the Cistercian order counted 350 communities and at the end of the Middle Ages, it boasted 742 spread all over Europe.

# ROUSSILLON

Roussillon, the Roman *Vicus Russulus*, clings to a rocky spur, between the valleys of the Imergue and the Coulon. Ever since antiquity, this region has been one of the most important centres for the mining of ochre.
Ochre is a composite of iron oxide and clay sand and ranges in color from a golden white to light yellow, from saffron yellow to brilliant red to burnt terracotta: as many as 17 shades! In ancient times it was also used to make cave drawings. A flourishing trade with the Orient arose above all at the end of the eighteenth century, spurred by Jean-Etienne Astier, with the material transported on muleback as far as Marseilles. Then, as the centuries passed, the quarries were exploited less and less, until the advent of synthetic colors marked the end of this flourishing local industry.

There is however a legend related to the extraordinary aspect of this area and it narrates of the secret love between Guillaume de Cabestang, a page and troubador, and Sermonde, the wife of Raymond d'Avignone, lord of Roussillon at the end of the 12th century, a love that blossomed during the frequent hunting excursions of the lord. When he discovered what had happened, he invited the page to go hunting, killed him, cut off his head and tore out his heart. Back at the castle, he had the heart cooked and served to his unsuspecting wife. Upon learning that she had eaten her lover's heart, Sermonde, crazed by horror and pain, ran out of the room to the highest part of the rock where she threw herself into the void. It is said that the two unhappy lovers were buried together and that their blood tinged all the surrounding land red.

*Panorama.*

*An instrument for astronomical measurements on the belvedere of Roussillon.*

*The phantasmagoric play of colours of the ochre earth in the village of Roussillon.*

The Saint-Jacques hill seen from Cavaillon.

The Roman arch and two views of the Cathedral.

# CAVAILLON

Nowadays Cavaillon is one of the most important farming areas in France; it is especially famous for its melons. Once upon a time it was Cabellio, or rather «Cabellio colonia in Cavaribus», as Ptolemy called it, and it was the ancient capital of Cavari. Neolithic remains have been brought to light on Saint-Jacques hill, known in ancient times as Mont Caveau; in fact, during the 4th century, the Cavari Celts settled there, attracted by its exceptional strategic position, and built a fortified town. The fact that it was built at the confluence of the Durance and the Coulon also contributed to the growth of the town. Strabo narrates how at the time the Durance could be crossed on rudimental rafts consisting of bags made out of animal hides filled with air. Cavaillon is steeped in history. Its Gallic origins can be seen from the communication trench cut out of the rock, where the tracks of the cart-wheels are still visible. On the site dedicated to the worship of St. Véran, Bishop of Cavaillon during the VI century, stands **Notre Dame and St. Véran Cathedral**, built between 1115 and 1125 and consecrated in 1251 by Pope Innocent IV; its original Romanesque style was transformed into Gothic and the church was then enlarged by adding side chapels.

In Roman times, a short distance away was the Forum, where the *decumanus* used to cross the *cardo* passing under a **Roman arch** which, in 1880, was dismantled stone by stone and rebuilt on Place François Tourvel. The fact that the rear façade of the arch is completely unadorned leads one to believe that it was originally erected against another building. It must have been constructed according to a square plan, with pillars at the corners; nowadays, it consists of two fully centred arches and is distinguished by rich decoration on the pillars, where one can glimpse birds and butterflies among the entangled acanthus leaves.

One can enjoy an exceptional view from the heights of Saint-Jacques hill, where one's gaze can sweep as far as the heights of the Lubéron. Here stands a small 12th century church with a single nave and apse, next to a hermitage which has been inhabited since the 14th century.

A view of the Montagne du Lubéron and a panorama of the valley that stretches out at the foot of the village of Lacoste.

The elegant small palace known as Le Castelet in the village of Ménerbes.

# LUBÉRON

From a geological and geographic point of view, Lubéron is a far flung chain of limestone hills, whose formation is more or less contemporary with that of the Pyrenees, around forty million years ago.

The Montagne du Lubéron stretches from Cavaillon up to the valley of Manosque and is cut into two unequal parts by the fault of Lourmarin: the Grand Lubéron and the Petit Lubéron. The valley that marks the northern border is bathed by the Cavalon and the Coulon, the southern valley by the Durance. It varies greatly in altitude: on the west a softly rolling series of hills is barely eight hundred meters high, while on the east the highest peak is that of the Mourre Nègre, with its 1125 meters. Consequently, the landscapes of the Lubéron are also highly varied. On the northern slopes, picturesque villages climb up and cling to the spurs of rock, each one marked by its bell tower, each one with its castle which dominates above and which bears witness to a past of wars, sieges and raids. The southern slope, on the contrary, is the softer, more intimate side, better prepared to receive the green spaces which open in the lazy curves of the Durance.

## MÉNERBES

The ancient Machovilla mentioned by Gregory of Tours rises up on the peak of a hill. A citadel of solid Calvinist faith, it was besieged from September 1577 to December 1578 by a Catholic army of almost ten thousand men. It was the Catholics who built the present castle in 1581. What is now known as **Le Castelet**, just below a lovely church in early Gothic style, is more of a patrician dwelling than a real fortification.

Ménerbes is also important because one of the rare dolmens in upper Provence is to be found here, along the road that leads to Bonnieux. Known as La Pitchuno it weighs at least ten tons.

*Ménerbes - Panorama of the village, a detail of the city wall and the Gothic church.*

*Lacoste - Two pictures of the village and a view of the ruins of the castle.*

# LACOSTE

Situated opposite Bonnieux, it can be said that Lacoste is one of the most typical and interesting villages of the entire region, with its narrow steep cobbled streets, elegant houses with sculptured portals and graceful windows, its slender towers. Yet much of its fame derives from the fact that the «divin marchese» de Sade lived in its **castle**, now in ruin. De Sade had fled from Paris in 1771 and found refuge here till 1778, in an exile which included frequent flights to Marseilles or Italy. The castle, which served as model in the «Hundred and twenty days of Sodoma», in 1778 still had almost fifty rooms and a drawbridge. A superb panorama of the region is to be had from the summit.

# BONNIEUX

The ancient name of this village, which dominates all the surrounding landscape, was Mitrone. Thanks to its position, as time passed it gained control not only of the access to the valley of the Durance, but protected it from the raids of brigands and other varied scourges typical of the times, not least of which was the plague. A church, now shaded by an enormous cedar tree, was built on top of the hill on the site of an ancient oppidum.

Not far from Bonnieux is one of the best preserved Gallo-Roman bridges in the area, the hog-backed **Pont-Julien**, 68 meters long, with three arches that span the Calavon, and which united north Italy to Arles via the Alps.

# APT

It was here, before the Roman conquest, that a Celtic-Ligurian tribe, the Vulgientes, lived before the Roman conquest. They made it their capital and called it Hath. After the conquest in 40 B.C., the city became Apta Julia and was equipped with a forum, baths and an amphitheatre.

Its fame rests on the fact that the **cathedral**, founded by St. Auspicius, bishop and martyr, on the site of a Roman temple, preserves a relic of St. Anne, mother of the Virgin. The so- called «veil of Saint Anne», which was discovered during a miracle on Easter day in 776 in the presence of Charlemagne, is actually a Muslim fabric dating to the 11th century, given to some Crusaders from Apt by a Fatimite caliph.

# ANSOUIS

Of all the stories and traditions of this land, the one concerning the castle of Ansouis is one of the loveliest and most moving. It was here in this castle that St. Elzéar and his wife Delphine of Sabran lived their lives of holiness and chastity. Delphine, who had made a vow of chastity, agreed to marry only if her husband made the same vow. He consented and the two lived a life of mortification and charity, realizing prodigies and miracles, to the point where Elzéar (who died in 1325), was canonized by Pope Urban V.

The **castle**, austere and architecturally unified, was remodelled twice: the French gardens are truly splendid, arranged harmoniously on several levels with cypresses, pines and boxwood. The castle is now inhabited and tasefully furnished by its present owners.

The former hall of Justice of the barons of Ansouis has been transformed into a church and can be seen not far from the castle, with a somber entrance surmounted by embrasures.

*Bonnieux - Panorama of the village.*

*Apt - A view of the cathedral.*

*Ansouis - General view of the village, the façade of the church and the entrance to the castle.*

*Lauris - A view of the eighteenth century Château.*

*Cadenet - Amy's statue featuring André Estienne, the drummer boy of Arcole.*

# LAURIS

Unfortunately the two circles of walls which in the past defended the village of Lauris no longer exist, although the village is still dominated by a solid 18th-century **castle**. The streets of the village are still lined by the lovely façades of the patrician dwellings, the decorated portals, the fountains.

# CADENET

Capital of the Ligurian tribe of the Caudellenses, the town of Cadenet is the homeland of the famous drummer boy of Arcole, whose statue, by Amy, stands in the main square.

The episode has become famous and is mentioned in all history books: in 1796, the French revolutionaries and the Austrians were fighting for the bridge of Arcole and the results were highly uncertain. The young drummer boy, at this point, swam the river Alpone and, once across, sounded the charge. The Austrians thought they were being attacked from behind and were surrounded by the enemy, and fled precipitiously leaving the bridge in French hands.

*Lourmarin - A general view of the village and the imposing Castle.*

# LOURMARIN

The impression of this village as seen from the road that skirts it is one of great serenity and beauty: a bell tower emerges almost timidly from the green of the small valley, and then the red roofs of the houses begin to appear here and there. The fine Renaissance Château stands almost alone, as if it were keeping watch over the village. The first nucleus dates to the middle of the 16th century. It was completely restored in 1920 by Robert Laurent-Vibert, who furnished it with antique Provençal and Spanish furniture and paintings of Italian school.

This territory was inhabited as far back as Neolithic times, and then in the Gallo-Roman period. The Benedictines of Saint-André de Villeneuve founded the first nucleus of the village.

The small cemetery of Lourmarin contains the tomb of Albert Camus, one of the greatest modern writers, Nobel Prize for literature in 1957, who found peace and serenity here in his later years until he died in an automobile accident on January 4th, 1960.

*The elegant façade of the abbey of Silvacane.*

# ABBEY OF SILVACANE

Together with Sénanque and Le Thoronet, Silvacane is one of the three great Cistercian abbeys in Province (the so-called three Cistercian sisters of Provence) and perhaps the most elegant of the three.

The name derives from the site where it was built, a forest of canes (*silva cannorum*): it was indeed an unhealthy swampy zone where a small group of Christians settled in the Middle Ages so they could live a life of penitence and work. Around 1144 Cistercian monks (an order founded by Robert but whose greatest figure was Bernard de Clairvaux) arrived from Morimond. The abbey, which seems to have been finished by 1193, immediately enjoyed the favours and benefices of the noble families and lords of Provence. The abbey and its estates grew at such a rate that in 1289 the Benedictines of Montmajour conspired to separate Silvacane from the Cistercian order. The ensuing struggle was bitter, and after being plundered by bands of local squires, a terrible cold spell in the winter of 1364 killed off the olives and vineyards which constituted the wealth of the abbey. By the early

15th century the church was almost abandoned and monastic life was no longer carried on. Restoration was not begun until 1949.

Despite the fact that this church is fully in line with the statutes of the Cistercian order which prohibited all decorative and architectural ornamentation that might distract the faithful from prayer, the impression is one of extreme grace, harmony and elegance.

The **exterior** is divided into three parts, marked by broad buttresses. Inside, the nave and aisles are separated by solid cruciform piers with attached half columns. The four square chapels open off the transept in pairs. The crossing of the transept is surmounted by a square bell tower: the Cistercian order prohibited the erection of stone bell towers, but in this case permission was given because the violence of the mistral and the danger of fire would have made wood useless.

The convent buildings, such as the refectory, the chapter hall and the library, open off the cloister, which also has robust square piers which support round headed arches.

# SALON-DE-PROVENCE

The origins of ancient *Salo* may go back to the oppidum of St.-Pierre-de-Canon, where Roman coins dating to the first century have come to light. Situated at the edge of the plain of the Crau, Salon became an important traffic node on the Via Aurelia and a crosspoint in the salt road during Roman times.

In the medieval period the raising of goats and sheep began in the plain which surrounds Salon. A parallel development was that of trade in oil, wool and skins, which led to the creation of the first important fairs and markets. In the 16th century King Henri II's engineer, Adam de Craponne, brought the waters of the Durance through a canal up to Salon. The canal, inaugurated on April 20, 1559, made the Crau fertile and from that time on olives, pastures and vineyards became an integral part of the landscape of Salon.

The prosperity of Salon increased with the passing of centuries: trade in oil became important to the point that Salon also became one of the most important producers of soap, with eventually as many as twelve factories. Signs of its ancient wealth have not completely disappeared: all one has to do is wander through the narrow streets or stop at a table in a shady square.

Passing through the 17th century **Clock-tower**, with its tower topped by a belfry in wrought iron, we enter the labyrinth of streets and lanes which form the nucleus, the heart of Salon and which lead us up to a small square closed theatrically by the Romanesque **church of Saint-Michel**, with a carved tympanum and bell towers lightened by arches.

After a few steps, at the top of a flight of stairs which climbs up the rock of Puech, stands the **Château de l'Empéri**, built between the 10th and 14th century, enlarged in the 16th and transformed into a barracks in the 19th. Today it houses the *Musée d'Art et d'Histoire Militaires*, with its fine and particular collections of art and military history: in the Renaissance court of honour the festival of Salon is held each year in summer.

*Salon-de-Provence - The Tour de l'Horloge.*

*The Château de l'Empéri and two views of the Museum housed inside.*

## CHÂTEAU MUSÉE DE L'EMPÉRI

Perched on an impressive pedestal of rock, the Château de l'Empéri, one of the most imposing monuments in Provence, dominates the town below. Fief of the archbishops of Arles under the suzerainty of the Germanic emperors of the Holy Roman Empire (hence is name), it was built between the 10th and 14th centuries, and completed with a fine arcaded gallery in the 16th century.

The museum houses the Raoul and Jean Brunon Collections, the richest in France, now state-owned, devoted to French military history since Louis XIV. The fine architecture of the 30 rooms of the château have, in their diversity, made it possible to exhibit the 10,000 authentic pieces to their best advantage: colourful uniforms, firearms, historical standards, paintings, decorations, etc. More than 140 mannikins, 18 of which on horseback, illustrate the magnificent uniforms of three centuries of French history in spectacular scenes. A large part of the visit is devoted to the exceedingly important Napoleonic period.

The quality and wealth of the collections make this one of the ten most important museums of military history in the world.

# MUSÉE GREVIN DE LA PROVENCE

In Place des Centuries, across from the fine flight of stairs which leads to the Château de l'Empéri, stands the Wax Museum of Provence, which in sixteen scenes narrates the story of this region, from 600 B.C. up to the present. The first scene is set in Marseilles in 600 B.C., when the Greeks founded the first cities on the Mediterranean coast, including Niece, Arles and Antibes. Then on to the year 102 B.C. when the Roman general Marius, launched the final attack against the Teutons near the Sainte Victoire mountain. Then comes Glanum (and we are now in the year 10 B.C.), an important trading center on the Via Aurelia and, in scene IV, to Saintes-Maries-de-la-Mer. The history of Provence gradually unfolds before our eyes, with its events and literary personages, first among whom that of Petrarch's vision at Fontaine de Vaucluse in 1337 when, after Laura's death, the idealized woman appears next to the «clear fresh and sweet waters». Still another episode, still another famous personage appears in scene XIII: the Crau in 1870, with Mireille, the heroine of Mistral's romance. And together with Mistral, we have the other great author of Provence, Daudet.

*Wax Museum of Provence - Famous personages and episodes in the history of the region: Laura and Petrarch, Mireille and Alphonse Daudet.*

*The House of Nostradamus - A detail of Nostradamus in one of the scenes recreated inside the Museum, and, below, the entrance to the house where he lived and died.*

## HOUSE OF NOSTRADAMUS

An interesting museum has been installed in the house in which Michel de Notredame, known as Nostradamus, lived from 1547 to July 2, 1566, when he died. Ten scenes and an exhibition of objects and ancient documents explain and illustrate the outstanding moments in the life of this famous personage, a true man of the Renaissance in his insatiable thirst for truth and knowledge.

Michel de Notredame was born in Staint-Rémy-de-Provence on December 14, 1503. Physician, expert in astrology and soothsaying, he was already famous for his remedies and recipes against the plague and other illnesses when he moved to Salon in 1547. Many illustrious personages of the time, attracted by his mysterious and occult sciences, came to consult him, first among whom, in 1564, Catherine de'Medicis, with her son Charles IX.

In 1555 he published his first «Centuries» and three years later the complete edition of the prophesies was issued. The «Centuries» are written in the form of quatrains in ten syllables in 16th-century French. They are a sort of prophetic description of the future: every event is always indicated exactly in space, but never in time, so that every one can interpret the enigmatic and mysterious verses as he pleases.

# MUSÉE DE SALON ET DE LA CRAU

Housed in a fine 19th century house in Provençal style, this museum illustrates the history of the region and its old traditions in the various sectors. There are collections of archeology, ethnography, natural history. On the ground floor is a relief, fifteen meters square, with a play of lights and sounds, which narrates the history of the territory from its farthest origins. Then various rural and domestic activities from the zone of the Crau are represented, as well as religious art and a few examples of painting of the Provençal school of the 19th century: above all works by Théodore Jourdan (1833-1908), a master at evoking in his sweeping canvasses the simplicity and freshness of a world that has unfortunately passed away.

On the upper floor, the Natural History section has a collection of over seven hundred examples of birds and other animals, all shown in the setting of a diorama.

On the same floor there is the interesting section dedicated to the making and selling of soap of Marseilles. Strictly regulated by Colbert's Edict of 1688, the soap industry was flourishing and lively for a long time. Various examples of soap with the manufacturer's trade mark are on exhibit, as well as labels, machines to cut the soap, prints and reconstructions which show how it was cut and so on.

*Museum of Salon and of the Crau - An oil painting by Théodore Jourdan entitled «Chevrière et son âne», painted in 1904, and two cases with objects and documentation regarding the soap industry.*

# MARSEILLES

The city, founded by the Greeks in 600 BC, grew up around the natural bay that was also the first site of human settlement in the area. Still today, the **Old Port** accounts for a goodly part of the city's charm, with its fishermen, fish market at the Quai des Belges, and its quaint restaurants. The quay, built in 1512 and enlarged in 1855, is a favorite promenade for the Marseillais.

The **forts of Saint-Jean** and **Saint-Nicolas** stand guard over the entrance to the Old Port; the first was built to defend the city's oldest, North Gate, while the second, more recent fortification was never used for defensive purposes and is today one of the most beautiful citadels of Provence.

Construction of the **Abbey of Saint-Victor**, one of the city's oldest religious edifices, was begun in the 5th century on the tombs of the Christian martyrs (among which, most probably, that of Saint Victor). Over the centuries it was enlarged and modified, beginning with the construction of the upper church and the naves and continuing through the fortification ordered by Pope Urban V to the 20th century restoration. The abbey has always been a site of veneration of the martyrs and is still the center of the Candlemas celebrations, to which is linked the legend of the navettes, traditional cookies in the form of boats that Provencal folklore identifies with the ships that brought the first evangelizers to the region.

**La Major** is the name given to two churches built on a single site. The older, Romanesque building dates to the 5th century, although it was rebuilt in the 11th and 12th centuries after the Saracen raids. The other, begun in the mid 19th century by the architects Vandoyer and Espérandieu, is in Byzantine style and adorned with precious stones and Italian marbles; this huge church is now the cathedral of Marseilles.

The church of **Saint-Vincent-de-Paul** is another 19th century work raised on the site of the former church of the Reformed Augustine monks; with its Gothic spires, it is an essential part of the view from the **Canebière**,

*An aerial view of the Old Port with the Palais du Pharo in the foreground.*

*An aerial view of Notre-Dame-de-la-Garde.*

a boulevard about one kilometer in length that links the church with the Old Port. The boulevard is a city promenade and home to a picturesque flower market and the creche statues fair during the Christmas season.

**Notre-Dame-de-la-Garde** was built by the architect Espérandieu on the site occupied for centuries the Chapel de la Garde (the name comes from the height on which a guard was posted), a site of pilgrimage. Francis I had a new chapel, consecrated in the 16th century, built on the site, and today's church was built in Romanesque-Byzantine style and consecrated in 1864.

La Bonne-Mère, as it is called by the Marseillais, stands against the skyline and dominates the city from above.

The City Hall, overlooking the Old Port, was built in pink stone in the 17th century. The main facade is embellished by a bust of Louis XIV and the north facade by an outstanding sculpted wooden portal (1679).

The Opéra, inaugurated in 1787, was designed in the Neo-Greek style in vogue at that time; following the fire of 1919 it was rebuilt in the same style. The interiors, instead, are furnished in the style in vogue in the 1920s.

*The Fort of Saint-Jean and the Fort Saint-Nicolas.*

*Notre-Dame-de-Confession, also known as the Black Virgin, in the abbey of Saint Victor.*

*The La Major cathedral.*

Two of the oldest homes of old Marseilles are the Maison de Cabre, built in the 16th century, and the so-called "Diamond House" named thus after the singular cut of the stones that face the facade. Built in 1570, this maison is now home to the Musée du Vieux Marseilles.

Another interesting building is the Hospice de la Vieille-Charité, construction of which lasted from the mid-17th to the mid-18th century. Built to shelter the city's poor, it is delineated by vaulted galleries and three rows of arches and now includes a new chapel in Baroque style. The hospice is today the seat of a number of organizations and associations.

Place De Gaulle is home to the Stock Exchange Building, a Second Empire construction dating to the mid 19th-century. The facade is embellished with the emblems of the merchant marine, astronomy, agriculture, commerce, and industry. Besides the activities linked to the stock exchange, the building is also home to the Musée de la Marine. Another building in pure Second Empire style is **Palais Longchamp**, a mid-19th century work by the architect Espérandieu designed to celebrate the construction of the Marseilles canal. The two wings of the castle, united by two colonnaded galleries, host the Museum of Natural History and the Museum of Fine Arts. The park setting, with its gardens and water-

*A view of the Canebière, the Palais Longchamp, the charming port of Vallon des Auffes, and the velodrome.*

falls, is a pleasant place for a relaxing stroll or recreational activities. Vestiges of ancient Marseilles include the Crinas, a part of the Greek walls preserved in later reconstructions, and an important archaeological site opened in the late 1960s not far from the Old Port and the Canebière.

Offshore of Marseilles are four islands, the smallest of which, the Château d'If, was fortified by Francis I in 1524. In the late 16th century a circle of walls enclosing all of the island, a church, and a guardhouse were built. Since the 17th century, the Château d'If has been the place of detention of illustrious prisoners, not least of whom the hero of Alexander Dumas' The Count of Montecristo. The two **Frioul Islands**, today united, abound in arid rocks and sheer-walled inlets - and the surrounding waters are a divers' paradise.

*A panoramic view of one of the Frioul islands, and aerial view of the Château d'If, and a stretch of beach at Espace Borely.*

# THE CALANQUES

Created by the water and wind erosion that over the centuries has modeled the rocks, the area known as the Calanques is today an extraordinary landscape with needle-sharp crests, crags, rocky spurs dropping sheer into the sea, and small hidden beaches - all along the stretch of coast running from Cassis to Marseilles. The Aleppo pine is dominant and sometimes flanked by oak and ash, while myrtle, rosemary, thyme, and the strawberry tree complete the vegetation. The fauna counts many species of birds, insects, and mammals.

Archaeological finds have proven that this coast was the site of human settlements in remote times. Today, diving enthusiasts come from all over the world to admire the sunken natural and archaeological wonders of the area: the **Grotte de Cosquer**, for example, discovered in 1991, contains rock-paintings dating to 20,000 years ago. The visitor can take any one of the many walking tour itineraries through these areas, which are not always reachable by car. The trails wind among the rocks along the coast in a wild environment fraught with suggestion.

Those localities of the Calanques best known and most appreciated by tourists are **Port-Pin**, **En-Vau**, the area around **Morgiou**, **Sormiou**, and finally **Cassis**, with its sheltered small port, east of Cap Canaille and west of the last rocky promontory of the Gardiole in an extremely beautiful natural setting.

*On the following page, the Calanques at En-Vau and at Morgiou, placid well-sheltered harbors, and an aerial view of the Calanques with Port-Pin in the foreground and Port-Miou behind.*

*The port of Cassis.*

*Place de la Libération with the Fontaine de la Rotonde.*

# AIX-EN-PROVENCE

In the 4th century B.C. western Lower Provence was occupied by a Celtic-Ligurian confederation, whose political and religious capital was the oppidum of Entremont. The tribes that felt themselves most threatened by this alliance appealed to the Romans for help, and it is for this reason that the Consul, Caius Sextus Calvinus, attacked and destroyed Entremont in 123 B.C. In the following year, in order to reinforce his conquests, the consul rightly decided to create a camp with entrenchments around some thermal springs which were already known in the area. This continually developing centre took the name Aquae Sextiae, and it was this city that was to become Aix-en-Provence.

Twenty years later, when the Teutons were marching on Italy, they were stopped in this area by the Roman army led by Marius. Rather, more exactly, according to tradition, the battle took place in 102 B.C. at the very foot of the elevation that was later to be called Mont St. Victoire. Marius' victory over the barbarians had great repercussions: many Provençal families formed the habit of calling one of their sons Marius, in his memory and honour. Aix was already capital of Gallia Narbonensis II, and was later the seat of an archbishop, when, from the 12th century on, it became «capital» as the Counts of Provence held a sophisticated literary and artistic court there. Despite the difficult trials that the city underwent (raids by bands of irregular soldiers, the terrible epidemic of the Black Death in 1348), the pre-eminence of Aix over the rest of the region was to continue for more than two centuries, reaching its peak in the 15th century under the famous «bon roi René.»

René d'Anjou, married to Isabelle de Lorraine and, in a second marriage, to Joan of Laval, spoke Greek, Latin, Italian, Hebrew, and Catalan; he wrote music and he painted; he had studied mathematics, jurisprudence and geology; he was a great traveller and went to Bourgogne, Flanders and Naples (where he was king from 1348 to 1442), to Florence and to Lombardy. Beneath him the city expanded and was made more beautiful; his patronage opened the doors of the court to many artists (the most famous was Nicolas Froment), festivals, games and tournaments were organized. His death, at 72 in 1480, almost marked the end of an era. Not completely so because, after the unification of Provence with France in 1486, Aix still retained a considerable autonomy and certain privileges; in fact the governor who represented the king resided here and the States General also met here after Louis XII had created the Parliament in 1501. During the 19th century Aix received a severe blow both from the events of the Revolution and the continuous development of Marseille as a port. The famous university which had been created in the 15th century by Louis II was reduced to the Faculties of Literature and Law and further, a Court of Appeal took the place of the Parliament. But this did not make Aix any the less attractive to artists, literati and poets. The lively centre of civic life today, the **Cours Mirabeau**, commemorates in its name the great writer and man of politics Gabriel-Honoré, Count of Mirabeau. Here in Aix he married, was divorced and was elected to the States General in 1788. The count had an enormous head, a face marked by smallpox, a rather corrupt and dissolute private life, so much so that he was known to his family as «Mirabeau de la Bourrasque» or «de l'Ouragan;» he distinguished himself by his extreme cleverness, his lively speech and his extraordinary political acumen. Aix dedicated this marvellous, shady avenue with spreading plane trees hundreds of years old to him. It was laid out in the 17th century on the site where the city ramparts had stood. There are three fountains along the avenue (the central one gushes thermal water at 34°), along one side there are the elegant façades of the aristocratic palaces and of the old hôtels; their entrances are richly sculpted and the balconies are in wrought iron, supported by caryatids, atlases and bunches of fruit. The other side of the avenue is made up of one shop after another, of book-shops and cafés. One of them is famous enough to equal Florian in Venice or Flore in Paris: this is the Café des Deux-Garçons; famous personalities from the literary and artistic world went there, from Emile Zola and Giraudoux to Jouvet, Cendrars and Cocteau. Of the many who remembered Aix («... il fait bon vivre à Aix...» wrote Jacques Lachaud), one always carried with him the memory and the images of his native city: this was Paul Cézanne who was born here in 1839 and, after various travels that took him far away, he returned to die here in 1906. For his entire life the great painter celebrated Aix, evoking its colours and its unparalleled light. Today it is possible to tread the

*A view of the Cours Mirabeau.*

*The Fontaine d'Albertas, of 1912, in the square of the same name, seen at night.*

*The façade of the Cathedral of St. Sauveur.*

*Interior of the Cathedral of St. Sauveur.*

*The Baptistery inside St. Sauveur.*

path of Cezanne, to visit his birthplace at no. 2 rue de l'Opéra, his father's hat shop at no. 55 Cours Mirabeau, and the studio in rue Boulegon where the artist died. Apart from these picturesque past events there are also the monuments of Aix, the most important of which is the cathedral: **St. Sauveur**. It was classified in 1739 as an «ugly and unsymmetrical church» by Charles de Brosses, well known as the «Président de Brosses.» And, in truth, the church is unsymmetrical because it contains all the different styles, but it certainly is not ugly, rather, in its extreme lack of symmetry and the superimposition of different styles and periods lies its beauty, or at least its charm. Tradition has it that it was built on the ruins of a temple dedicated to Apollo. The construction was begun in 1285 by Archbishop Rostang de Noves: the plan is that of a Latin cross (a nave with five spans, a transept and an apse), though it is highly deformed. By contrast with the grim bulk of the Romanesque church alongside, the façade of St. Sauveur stands out for its fantastic, flamboyant Gothic style. The buttresses are decorated with niches and with pinnacles which flank the very lovely double doors of the entrance porch; they were done by Jean Guiramand of Toulon, with sculpture depicting the Prophets of Israel and the Sibyls. On the left stands the bell-tower which was begun in

The fine Romanesque cloister inside St. Sauveur.

The Cathedral of St. Sauveur houses the famous
Triptych of the Burning Bush, one of the finest works
by Nicolas Froment.

Exterior of the church of Ste.-Marie-Madeleine.

1323; it is made up of two tapering, superimposed
parts, the upper being octagonal. The interior contains
some real artistic masterpieces: particularly the
**Baptistery** which dates from the end of the 4th and the
beginning of the 5th centuries. Like all the other bap-
tisteries of the Merovingian age this one has an octagonal structure and was made using material from an
earlier building, seen here in the eight columns, six of
green marble and two of granite with Corinthian capitals, which came from a Roman temple. In the centre
of the building an octagonal bath has been discovered
in which baptism by immersion for adults took place.
The **Cloister**, on the other hand, is Romanesque with
small round arches supported by small twin, marble
columns; it is marked by an exceptional lightness due
to the lack of reinforcing piers which do not therefore
interrupt the line of the columns. It dates from between
1160 and 1180 and imitates both the architecture and
iconography of the cloister of St. Trophime in Arles,
even though the latter is very much larger. The capitals
of the columns are decorated in different ways, the
sides facing the garden have plant motifs and the sides
facing inwards have human subjects. Of all the works
of art, however, the famous *Triptych of the Burning
Bush* predominates. It was completed around 1476 by
Nicolas Froment for King René, whose portrait, together with Sts. Anthony, Maurice and Magdalen appears on the left wing, while on the right wing are the
portraits of his wife, Joan of Laval, with saints John,

*Church of Ste.-Marie-Madeleine: the Triptych of the Annunciation.*

*Wooden statue of the Madonna and Child inside the Church of Ste.-Marie-Madeleine.*

*Below, the fountain of the Four Dolphins, of 1667; the fountain of Pascal, located in Cours Sextius; the 17th century fountain of the Trois Ormeaux.*

Nicholas and Catherine. In this altarpiece Nicolas Froment has given expression to the great Provençal style in its best and most noble form: the planes are well defined and the composition is solemn and monumental. Yet, some points, such as the minute care given to the drawing of the details and the attention given to the background landscape, bear an undoubtedly Flemish imprint. If this sacred architectural complex takes the first place for the works of art it con-

tains, the first place for the oldest must go to another church, that of **St. Jean-de-Malte**, which was the first Gothic building constructed in Aix. It was originally built on the plan of a Latin cross and was enlarged during the following centuries. It now contains the reconstructed sepulchre of the last Counts of Provence. St. Jean-de-Malte does not contain great works of art, but this is not the case with the **Church of Ste.-Marie-Madeleine.** Baroque in style and, as well as a painting

attributed to Rubens and a marble 18th century Virgin, it has the famous *Triptych of the Annunciation.*

This work, one of the most original of the age, was carried out between 1443 and 1445 for the cathedral of Aix. We know the name of the donor, the wealthy citizen Pierre Corpici, but not that of the artist. Several hypotheses have been put forward: perhaps it was Guillame Dombet who did the stained glass of the cathedral, or perhaps his son-in-law, Arnould de Catz. Only one fact is certain, the anonymous Master of the Annunciation knew the Flemish works of Jan van Eyck and of the Master of Flemalle very well indeed. Otherwise it would be impossible to explain the vigorous and monumental style, the knowledgeable use of warm light that sculpts the volumes and gives the whole composition an absolutely new dimension.

Aix also offers fine examples of non religious buildings, in whatever style they may be: the **Hôtel de Ville**, erected between 1562 and 1658 that has a **Gothic Clock Towe**r, is one example. Another is the **fountain of the Four Dolphins**, dating to 1667, with the superb 18th century palaces of Place des Quatre Dauphins as backdrop. And lastly, the **Méjanes Library**, one of the finest in France, with 300,000 volumes including the precious *Book of Hours*, illuminated by King René himself.

The 16th century Clock Tower.

The Fountain d'Espéluque, of 1618, located in Place Martyrs de la Resistence.

The former Archbishop's palace, now seat of the Tapestry Museum.

# ARLES

To describe Arles in a few pages is extremely difficult: its rich and glorious past, its many artistic beauties, its incredibly strange but musical language; the air that one breathes and the gay, happy and festive atmosphere of the city. One must live here to truly understand it.

Let us run through the important stages of its history. Its origins are lost in the mists of time: bones and flint heads which have been found in the surrounding areas testify that it was inhabited in very ancient times. At that time the region did not look as it appears today: the Mediterranean formed a deep estuary which has now disappeared and the whole area was covered by marshes created by the Rhône. The primitive peoples lived on some rocky islands which were, at most, 30 metres above sea level, and therefore more easily defended. The islet where Arles grew up was between the river and the Crau marshes. In fact, the Celts called this site Ar-laith, which means in front of the marshes, a name which the Romans later made into Arelate, the ancient form of Arles.

For many years Arles lived in the shadow of Marseilles, on which it was politically and economically dependent. Despite this Arles has important, positive factors in its favour: its important location on the road between Italy and Spain; its strategic position in the delta of the Rhône; roads which linked the Mediterranean basin with the other countries of Northern Europe, a fertile surrounding region which provided military supplies. It was only a matter of awaiting the right moment and this arrived when Marseilles sided with Pompey against Caesar. Caesar, besieging Marseilles from land and sea, received constant aid from Arles, including twelve ships which were supplied by the accomplished ship-builders in Arles in less than 80 days. In gratitude Caesar «promoted» this Provençal city, giving it the title, «Colonia Julia Paterna Arelatensis Sextanorum» and stationed the VI legion there. The title was very important because only the colonies founded by Caesar himself had the right to vaunt it. Arles then became the «Rome of the Gauls»: a rich city, enclosed with walls and united to the other bank of the river by a bridge of boats, there the residential city was laid out. There were pretty streets with pavements, the theatre, the arena, and public baths, made of marble with running water. Three canals supplied the

*Arles seen from the Rhône.*

at Arles. The Saracens also raided the city and devastated it twice, once in 842 and again in 869. It is true that in the 9th century Arles became the capital of a kingdom that included part of Provence and Bourgogne, but its also true that the city was no longer what it had once been. In 1239 it came under the direct control of the Counts of Provence and the city shared the history and destiny of the rest of the region. It was in an inferior position with regard to Aix and Marseille but, in the meantime, it was reasserting itself economically. Finally, with the arrival of the railways, the maritime commerce that there was along the Rhône also ceased; but the continuous advance and sanding up of the Rhône's delta cut it off from the sea for good. In Arles religious and civil buildings vie with each other in beauty and importance, they are sometimes close together as if to compete with each other.

For example, the **Hôtel de Ville**, with a 17th century façade, was developed around the Renaissance Tour de l'Horloge, from a design by Peytret, but the great Mansart gave it the finishing touch. On the tower there is a statue of the god, Mars, that the people of Arles call the «bronze man» because, even though it is not visible to someone standing below, it reflects the golden rays of the sun. And here is one of the finest works of art in Arles: the flat ceiling of the ground floor,

city with water; one supplied private houses, the second went to the public baths and the last to the fountains. Its port was very busy, particularly after the demise of Marseille: it attracted the ships coming from Asia and from Africa. The markets of Arles were very famous: oil and wine from Provence were exported. The artisans of Arles were renowned for their goldwork, weapons and fabrics. The Emperors chose it as their residence in Provence and Constantine himself stayed there.

It was also an important cultural centre where the sophist Favorinus had studied. In Christian times it became a great religious centre: seventeen councils were held here. The decline of Arles came with the barbarian invasions.

426, 430, 452, 454, 461, are the years in which the Visigothic hordes attacked the city. When the last Roman emperor Romulus Augustus died in 476, the way was open to the barbarians. The city finally collapsed in 480 when the Visigoths, led by Euric, having passed through Glanum, arrived

*The church of St. Trophime.*

supported by ten pairs of columns, an excellent example of architectural balance and structural perfection. Alongside the Hôtel de Ville, we can now admire the Romanesque beauty of the **Church of St. Trophime**, which is considered one of the most beautiful in Provence. According to one legend St. Trophime arrived in Provence from Palestine along with other monks of his order; in another version of the legend it is said that the saint, a disciple of St. Peter and St. Paul, came here from Rome. In any case he was the cousin of St. Stephen, the first Christian martyr, whose head he preserved when he was killed. During his work of converting Provence to the Christain faith St. Trophime stayed at Arles, and became its bishop. The first basilica in Arles, dedicated initially to St. Stephen, was destroyed in the first half of the 8th cen-

Church of Saint-Trophime, the portal: a detail of the lunette depicting the Last Judgment, and some of tp. he low-reliefs with figures of saints.

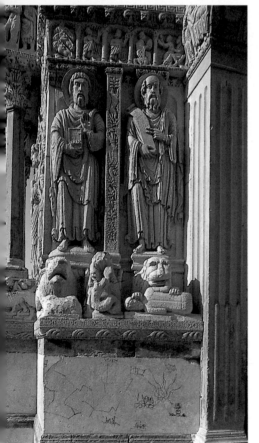

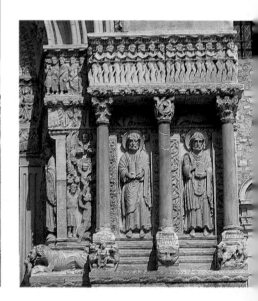

Church of Saint-Trophime, the facade by night and a
view of the apse with the high altar.

tury during the Saracen raids. Its reconstruction was
begun during the Carolingian age and on the 29th of
September 1152 the relics of St. Trophime were
solemnly translated and the church was dedicated. In
the cathedral, because by then it had become the cathedral, Frederick Redbeard received the royal crown
from archbishop Raymond de Bolène on the 30th July
1178: there also King René married Joan de Laval and,
in 1399, Louis II of Anjou married Jolanda of Aragon.
The façade (the lower part is Carolingian and the upper part is 12th century) is opened by the majestic
**twin portals.** They are similar to those of St. Gilles,
and were sculpted around 1180; with their perfect proportions and rich decoration they are similar to a Roman triumphal arch. There is a *Christ in glory* with the
symbols of the four evangelists in the lunette above the
architrave. Directly below we see twelve seated figures representing the *twelve apostles*. To the left of
Christ is a procession of naked figures in chains, these
are the souls of the damned being dragged to hell. On

His right the elect turn their faces to Him. Still further down there are more saints, each with his own symbol. The interior is severe, it has a nave and two aisles and ogival vaulting over the high nave and barrel vaulting in the aisles, which is very narrow. Many Christian sarcofagi are kept in the side and the radial chapels, dating from the 4th century. On one, which forms the altar-frontal in the chapel, the *Crossing of the Red Sea is* represented. And finally, the **cloister**, which we should not hesitate to call the most beautiful part of the church. The richness and liveliness of the sculptural decoration (here, as on the portal, the iconography is dedicated to the apostles) make it the most famous cloister in the area. Half Romanesque and half Gothic (the north and the east galleries date from the 12th century and the south and west galleries from the 14th), the cloister ably combines the two styles of the galleries, the Romanesque with truss vaults and the Gothic with ogival vaults. The capitals of the twin

*Two general views of the Cloister of St. Trophime.*

*Southeast part of the cloister with the well, whose rim was made of the base of an antique column from the Theatre.*

*The pier in the northwest corner of the cloister, with the representation of St. Trophime, first bishop of Arles.*

columns are all decorated, either with leaves and raceme or with scenes from the Old and New Testaments. Bas reliefs and statues are set into the pilasters which alternate with the columns: at the north-east corner the group of *St. Trophime, St. Peter, and St. John the Evangelist,* even though it is obviously inspired by antiquity it shows a perfection and newness of expression that is no longer antique and not even medieval, but without doubt anticipates the modern age. In a room that opens off the cloisters beautiful Aubusson tapestries are kept, dating from the 17th century, that depict the *Life of the Virgin;* there are others from Flanders from the same period representing the *History of the Jews.*

The **Arena** of Arles, like that of Nîmes, is among the most ancient of the Roman world: in fact, it may have been built during the reign of Hadrian. What impresses most is the size of the ellipse: it is 136 metres long and 107 high. It is able to contain 24,000 spectators, and is composed of two orders of arcades, each with 60 arches (the lower ones are Doric and the upper ones are Corinthian). One difference between this arena and that at Nîmes is the height of the wall around the central area, placed here obviously to protect the ringside spectators from any wild animals that may escape. Its history was very eventful and shared the same destiny as similar monuments in other cities whose materials were removed to build other houses and monuments. It was

sacked and turned into a fortress by the Saracens and was later occupied by the poor people of the city who made their homes there and also built two chapels. Beginning in 1825 it was restored and today Spanish-style corridas and the traditional festival of the guardians of the Camargue are held here. The shouts of the gladiators and the growling of wild beasts are no longer heard – rather the enthusiastic yells of the crowd that watches, for example, the local feast of the cockade; man and beast still face each other but no longer to kill or be killed but rather for the enjoyment of the public who find the Arena a superb and appropriate setting for the spectacle that they attend. Other local events take place in what remains of the **Theatre.** It must have been marvellous with its magnificent «frons scenae» decorated with statues and dominated by that of Augustus which was flanked by Diana (only

*A few views of the «cavea» of the Arena with details of the tiers around it.*

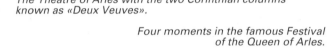

The Theatre of Arles with the two Corinthian columns known as «Deux Veuves».

Four moments in the famous Festival of the Queen of Arles.

the head of which has been found) and by the famous Venus of Arles, which was discovered on the 6th of June 1651. According to some the theatre was built around 30 B.C., according to others between 20 and 15 B.C., in any case during the times of Augustus. This monument has suffered more than any other in Arles from the ravages of time and man. Since the 5th century the fanaticism of Christianity was mostly to blame for its systematic destruction–its stone was used as building material for churches, private homes and defensive walls. Of its three arcaded levels all that remains today is the isolated Tour de Roland; on this the stage must have been situated and also the two columns named the «Deux Veuves,» the two widows. In this picturesque stone setting, covered with greenery, very important shows take place. For example, the annual July Festival in which the most famous names in the performing arts take part, from ballet dancers to opera singers, from violinists to actors; Arles has become for these people a compulsory step in their careers. There are also Folk Festivals, such as the **Festival of the Queen of Arles.** Groups from all over Provence participate in this, each dressed in their local costumes. But of all the women in regional costume its impossible to confuse the women of Arles with any

*Réattu Museum - Antoine Raspal (1738-1811): The Painter's Family.*

*Réattu Museum - Jacques Réattu (1760-1833): The Death of Alcibiades.*

*A detail of the internal court of the Arlaten Museum.*

others. Their dress, their bearing and their elegance make them stand out from the others. Severe and simple, yet at the same time full of grace and sumptuous the costume consists of a long, narrow skirt with three flounces of silk modelled and tied at the waist with organza and lace in a complicated play of pleats. The drapery continues over the chest, here it is called «la chapelle» (the chapel) as it was customary to hang a reliquary there – today a cross of silver or gold is placed here. The hair is always done up, the style of which changes according to age: the young girls wear lace knotted to form butterfly wings and the married women have a wide bow. Van Gogh immortalized these costumes of Arles dozens and dozens of times during his stay in the city, and they may also be seen in two of the city's museums: the **Réattu Museum** and the **Arlaten Museum.**

The first is situated in the old palace of the Grand Prior of the Knights of Malta, a fine example of Renaissance military architecture. When the property of the Order was sold during the Revolution it was bought by the painter Réattu who established his studio in the palace.

After his death it was inherited by his daughter who donated it to the city of Arles.

Many of Réattu's paintings are kept here, also those of his father, M.de Barreme, and his uncle, Antoine Raspal; there are also contemporary works of art including paintings by Picasso and sculpture by Zadkine. The second museum, the Arlaten Museum, was created by Frederic Mistral who, having received the Nobel Prize for literature in 1904, used the money to bring to life a museum that could offer a wide overview of Provençal history and folklore. The museum was laid out in the Gothic Hôtel de Castellane-Laval. In the courtyard there is the so-called Dodekatheion, an exedra of a small Roman temple. In the 33 rooms of the museum there are interesting documents about the costumes and the traditions of Provence, about local history and the various trade corporations, about the rites and the ethnography of the different parts of the region. There is also the reconstruction of the *interior of a house in the Camargue* with a scene from everyday life (on this occasion it is a *visit to a woman with a new-born child*) in which the people are dressed in the costumes of the age.

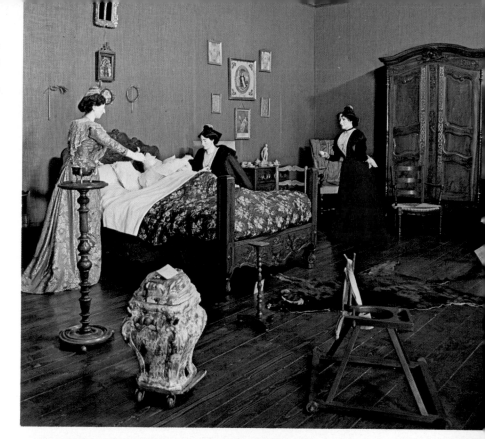

Arlaten Museum - The reconstruction of the bedchamber of a new mother shown receiving visits.

Arlaten Museum - The reconstruction of the interior of a house in the Camargue.

# ESPACE VAN GOGH

It may have been Toulouse-Lautrec's suggestion that brought Vincent van Gogh to the south of France in February of 1888. The light and colours of the region made a powerful impression on his sensitive soul and influenced his art.

The Espace Van Gogh, a recently created cultural centre dedicated to the artist, is located on the old hospital of Arles, where the Dutch painter stayed more than once on account of his frequent mental crises. The fine mediatheque and numerous exhibition rooms are centred around the court of the **Hôtel-Dieu**, restored by the city in the shapes and colours used by Van Gogh in the marvelous picture he painted in April 1889 when he was a patient there.

In Arles, where the artist remained until his voluntary recovery in the psychiatric hospital of Saint-Rémy, Van Gogh produced an incredible number of canvasses and drawings.

*Two pictures of the Espace Van Gogh, the cultural centre dedicated to the artist that has recently been installed in the old hospital where van Gogh was recovered for various months.*

*Two views of the evocative setting of Les Alyscamps.*

The final marvellous impression which we can take away from Arles is the **Alyscamps**, a famous and evocative place that has inspired poets, painters and writers since ancient times.

The name Alyscamps is a deformation of the term Elysian Fields; this is in fact an ancient necropolis which was already famous at the time of the Gauls. In the early centuries burials were made by the Phoenicians, the Celts, the Gauls and the Greeks! Then the Romans had their sepulchres placed along the Via Aurelia, at the entrance of the city. From the 4th century the necropolis became Christian and was considerably enlarged, so much so that at the end of the Middle Ages there were seventeen churches or chapels. The atmosphere of the place is so strong that Dante himself mentions it in the ninth canto of «Inferno»; according to a medieval legend the body of Orlando, after his death at Roncesvalles, was brought here. Ariosto in «Orlando Furioso» sets the great combat between Orlando and the Saracens here, beneath these hoary old trees, among these ancient stones. In November 1888 Vincent van Gogh came here to paint, together with his friend Gauguin; but they never chose the same subject, nor did they set their easels close together. The paintings that they produced are completely different one from the other: those by Gauguin are more delicate and sweeter while those by van Gogh give way to the strongest of emotions with the brightest of colours and rapid and vibrant brush strokes which are almost brutal. It was actually here in Arles that van Gogh's tragedy was to take place; having first tried to attack his friend Gauguin with a razor, immediately afterwards, closed in his room, being subject to a fit of madness he cut off his left ear. But in the peace of Alyscamps there was no presentiment of the impending tragedy. The ruin of Alyscamps began with the Renaissance when the nobles of Arles unfortunately got the terrible habit of giving at least a sarcophagus to their famous guests; naturally they chose the loveliest and the best sculpted that the cemetery could offer. The monks who were the guardians of the cemetery used the stones of the ancient sarcophagi to build their churches; its even said that Charles IX, who wanted to make a private collection of these sarcophagi, loaded so many of them onto a boat that it sank.

Man and progress (the construction of the railway cuts across the entrance to the avenue) have therefore unfortunately destroyed for the most part the sacredness of a place where time had stopped 2,000 years ago. But fortunately these have not put an end to the beauty of the place, the peace and tranquility of the necropolis where sadness is the only witness to its more glorious past.

The many coloured **Amadieu Pichot fountain** has a joyful appearance; the central medallions are the works of Paul Palze, an artist from Arles. The fountain

The picturesque Amadieu Pichot fountain, inaugurated in 1887.

The bridge of Langlois as van Gogh painted it in one of his four versions of this subject.

The Bridge of Langlois - Van Gogh painted four versions of this subject: this bridge, which joined Arles to Port-de-Bouc, was torn down in 1935 and has recently been rebuilt, in identical form, in memory of the great painter.

was inaugurated in April 1887, during the presidency of Mistral, and is dedicated to a famous citizen of Arles, the man of letters Amadieu Pichot. He was born here on the 3rd November 1795, but went while still very young to Paris, where he studied at the college of Juilly. He became a doctor of medicine in 1817. He always had a great passion for English literature and founded the *Revue Britannique* and in a book entitled *L'Arlesienne* he gathered together all the poetry inspired by the picturesque beauty of Arles. After he died, aged 80, his city wished to dedicate to him a moving testimony, the very colourful and happy fountain, placed at the intersection of two roads, which cordially welcomes whoever arrives in the city.

*A highly varied market takes place every Saturday morning on the Boulevard des Lices. Everything is sold here, from antiques to things that are simply old, from the typical Provençal fabrics to the dozens of herbs and spices for which the region is known.*

*An evocative sunset and a typical picture of the Camargue.*

# THE CAMARGUE

This enormous area of about 800 square kilometres that lies between the two arms of the Rhône and the sea, is occupied in the centre by the immense marsh of Vaccarès and is one of the most interesting in France. Since the most ancient times the Rhône delta has been like a gate, open onto the mysterious region of Gaul and, like all things unknown, dangers of all possible kinds were imagined. To Hesiod the delta was one of the three mouths of hell, together with the Po and the Rhine. One can truly say that it was the river that created this landscape: its course has undergone, during the centuries, infinite changes, changing at the same time the land through which it ran. Each year the river brings sand and silt to the sea thus causing the coast-line to advance by 10 to 50 metres each year. At the same time the sea is pushing inland and gains new ground. The town of Saintes-Maries-de-la-Mer, which in the Middle Ages was several kilometres from the coast, was 600 metres away in 1814 and is now washed by the sea. By the opposite process the lighthouse of Saint Louis, built in 1737 at the mouth of the Rhône, now rises in isolation, 5 kilometres away from the Mediterranean. This immense plain of marshes and bogs, of lagoons and sand, dominated by salt which impregnates water and land (despite this over 8000 acres are now covered with rice fields!) has always inspired painters and writers: the «Chants palustres» of Joseph d'Arbaud, the poetic descriptions of Alphonse Daudet, and its greatest poet, Fredéric Mistral, who set the tragic end of the protagonist of «Mirèio» here. Mistral described this flat, almost perfectly horizontal plain as having «Ni arbre, ni ombre, ni âme.» Its highest point, at Albaron, is four and a half metres; its lowest point, the bottom of the marsh of Vaccares, is one and a half metres below sea level.

From any point of view this huge flat territory is an incredible zoological and botanical reserve. In 1828 the *Société Nationale de Protection de la Nature et d'Acclimatation de France* set up, at Vaccarès, a natural park where hunting, fishing, or picking of plants and flowers was prohibited. In 1950 the Swiss scientist, Luc Hoffmann, who had decided to dedicate all his research to the Camargue, founded a biological station connected with the French CNRS, and committed himself to the study of birds, specializing in their migratory habits. Other than its incredibly rich flora, ranging from alofile plants to tamarisk, from daisies to asphodels and narcissi, there are about 400 species of animals, both migratory and sedentary. This area of

*A few characteristic aspects of the Camargue: the bulls, horses, cranes and pink flamingos are an integral part of the landscape of the Camarague.*

the Rhône is one of the largest and most important migratory stops in Europe; the passage of the pink flamingo is particularly fascinating. In 1969, 10,000 were sighted on their way from North Africa. The undisputed lord of the region is the «camargue» bull, *lou biòu* in the local dialect; its majestic line distinguishes it both when seen alone or in the middle of the herd, called a *manade*. The bull, branded with the name of its owner during what is known as the *ferrade,* is often the central character of special «corride» where, unlike Spain, it is not killed. Called the «course à la cocarde», the purpose of this contest is to get hold of a red cockade hung between the horns of the animal, using a multipronged hook.The prize is decided according to the number of cockades obtained. The constant companion of this small bull (in general it is about 1.35 metres to the withers) of very ancient origin (thought to descend from the *Bos taurus asiaticus* brought from Asia Minor by Attila's hordes) is the beautiful, white horse with incredible resistance (it is able to cover up to 50 kilometres in a day); the origins of this animal are also uncertain, possibly a descendent of the horse of the Solutrean or upper Paleolithic period, or perhaps imported by the Carthaginians, or the Moors or from Central Asia. Its counterpart is the keeper who has a long pole, called a *lou ferre,* and a characteristic outfit which relates him to the American cow-boy.

*The church of Saintes-Maries-de-la-Mer with the statues of the saints in its interior: above right is the figure of St. Sarah, with her dark skin, as she is carried in procession, and the two figures of Mary of James and Mary Salomé, in the niche inside the church.*

# SAINTES-MARIES-DE-LA-MER

According to a Provençal legend, around 40 A.D., at the time of the persecution and captivity of the Jews in Jerusalem, three women, together with other companions of the faith, were thrown into a boat without a sail, oars or food, and left to their fate on the waves. The women were Mary of James, the Virgin's sister; Mary Salomé, the mother of the apostles John and James the Major; and Sarah the Egyptian, the black servant of the two Marys. Their other companions were Lazarus, Mary Magdalene and Martha. Miraculously the boat landed on this shore where the women erected a small chapel dedicated to the Virgin. Then the disciples separated, some went to Tarascon, some to Marseilles and some to Aix to preach and convert. The two Marys and Sarah remained here until their deaths when the faithful looked after their remains which soon became objects of worship. These were preserved in the chapel which, by the middle of the 11th century, had become a church; fortified and included in the circle of walls it resembled a fortress, seen above all in the powerful apse. Among the first of the faithful were the nomads, Spanish and other gypsies who, from the middle of the 15th century had found the boundless space of the Camargue in tune with their eternal wanderings. They began to take part, in ever greater numbers, with ever increasing emotion, in the annual pilgrimages that culminated, as today, on the night of the 24th/25th May and on 22nd October. The statue of St. Sarah, for whom the gypsies have a special veneration, is carried in procession to the sea where it is immersed, while the colourful throng of gypsies from all over the world surround their protectress. The feast lasts 10 days, with horse races, the running of the bulls, the ferrades; it is an annual rendezvous for the nomads, the women from Arles in costume, and the bull herders from all over the Camargue...

# AIGUES - MORTES

On the boundaries of the Camargue, in a strange land-scape of lagoons and canals, is Aigues Mortes, with surprising medieval echoes. The dates in its history are few but important. 1240: Louis IX the Holy, who had no direct control over a port obtained this land from the monks of the abbey of Psalmody, in order to create a military base and embarcation port there for the Crusade that he had proclaimed. 1248: 38 ships which had set sail from Genoa were ready to leave from Aigues Mortes, reaching the sea through the narrow Grau Louis canal. 1270: Louis IX set out once again from Aigues Mortes (on the 7th Crusade) but, having arrived at Tunis, he died of the plague on the 25th August. 1421: the Hundred Years War. The Burgundians occupied the city by surprise and at-tacked the garrison, killing all the Armagnans that they found. They were thrown into the tower which was known afterwards as the Tower of the Burgundians. There were so many corpses that salt was sprinkled over them to avoid putrefaction: this gave rise to the expression «Bourguignon sale,» which was used in the text of a song. Aigues Mortes remained a wealthy city until the middle of the 14th century: then the sea re-ceded and the canal filled with sand. The construction in the 18th century of the Sète canal was the final blow to the port. From that time Aigues Mortes turned to vine-yards and to salt production.

Aigues Mortes is one of the finest examples of a forti-fied medieval city. It is completely surrounded by walls in the form of a quadrilateral; the walls are topped by parapets, and it has twenty castellated tow-ers and ten gates. It was built for Louis IX before he left for the Crusade of 1248; he employed the Genovese consuls Nicola Cominelli and Guglielmo Boccanegra, and it was completed by his son Philip III the Bold. Isolated on the north-west corner of the wall rises the **Tour de Constance**, a powerful, cylindrical keep, joined to the walls by a bridge; this also was used as a lighthouse in the days of Aigues Mortes' maritime activities. For 5 centuries it was also a prison: the Masters of the Templars, the Huguenots and political prisoners were held here. The most fa-mous prisoner was a woman, a stubborn supporter of the Protestant faith, who remained here for 38 years. It was she who carved on the stone wall of her cell the word «Résistez.»

*Two pictures which highlight the beauty and excellent state of preservation of the city wall of Aigues Mortes and a bird's-eye view of the city*

*The façade of the church of St. Gilles.*

# SAINT-GILLES

The town of Saint-Gilles, which today is a prospering agricultural centre in a plain rich with grapes and cereals, is an enigma as far as its ancient history is concerned. Was it a port? Was it perhaps the ancient Heraklea founded by the Phoenicians? It is difficult to say. At most we know that its ancient name was Vallis Flaviana. According to legend St. Egidius landed here one day in the 8th century; he was an Athenian abbot who, touched by grace, had given all his wealth to the poor and set sail in a ship; he then lived in a cave at the mouth of the Rhône. One day a deer, which brought him food, was being hunted by the son of the Visigothic king, Wambo, and fled to the hermit who, with a single gesture, stopped the arrow that was about to mortally strike the animal. The king of the Visigoths, impressed by the miracle, wished to know the saint personally and decided to found an abbey. St. Egidius then went to Rome to obtain recognition for its foundation. The pope gave him two marvellous carved

doors which the saint threw into the Tiber. The doors sailed down river, crossed the sea and sailed up the Rhône until they arrived at the saint's cave. St. Egidius was buried in the church which he built and became an object of worship. Both the abbey and the town that surrounded it long enjoyed the protection of the pope, the King of France and the Counts of Toulouse until, with the rise and propagation of the Albigensian heresy, these favours ceased.

On the 5th of January 1208 the papal legate, Peter of Castelnau, was murdered in front of the main door of the church by one of Raymond VI's attendants; Raymond was immediately ex-communicated. Only on the 29th of June the following year, after presenting himself naked to be whipped in the church and then prostrating himself on the tomb of the dead man, was Raymond of Toulouse pardoned.

In 1562 when the wars of religion were at their height, the abbey's monks were thrown into the well in the crypt and the church was burned. After 1622, when even the bell tower was demolished, all that remained was a church almost in ruins; fortunately the superb **façade** was saved, this is rightly considered the finest example of southern Romanesque sculpture. Its construction begun in 1180 and finished in 1240 actually involved three different schools: the central doorway, which is the oldest, by sculptors of the Toulouse school, artists from the Ile-de-France carried out the two side doorways and local artists brought the statues of the apostles on the forepart to completion.

Together with that of St. Trophime, in Arles, the façade of the church of Saint-Gilles is renowned in Provence and for the richness, the beauty and the opulent covering of sculpture over the whole of the front of the building it can truly compete with the great Gothic cathedrals of the north. Inside, the **crypt**, dating from about 1180, was originally covered with a cross vault. It is 50 metres long and 25 metres wide and still contains some of the ogival vaults which are among the oldest known in the whole of France. The choir is unfortunately in ruins, but in the stair of the **north bell tower**, it remains the famous «vis de Saint-Gilles».

A much restored Romanesque house is preserved alongside the church. According to tradition this is the **birthplace of Guy Foulque**, or Guido Fulconii, who was to be elected pope on the 5th of February, 1265,

*One of the bas-reliefs which decorate the church of St. Gilles and what remains of the winding staircase of the north bell tower.*

*A few pictures of the lovely abbey of Montmajour: below, left, the imposing Tour de l'Abbé, and, on the opposite page, above, a detail of the cloister, considered the finest in Provence after that of St. Trophime at Arles, and a view of the ruins of the abbey.*

# THE ABBEY OF MONTMAJOUR

Once marshes surrounded this hill, today rice is cultivated there. The hill's summit has always been considered a holy place and was first inhabited by prehistoric peoples, then by Celts and finally by the Romans. After the Saracen invasions Montmajour became a Christian burial-place. From a document dated the 7th October 949, it seems that a woman named Teucinda bought it in order to make a gift of it to a religious community. In any case, Louis the Large sent some monks there who dedicated themselves patiently to the cultivation of the marshes. Around the Christian cemetery, during the 10th century, a Benedictine monastery was put up. Its fortune grew rapidly, thanks also to a «pardon,» created in 1030, which took place every 3rd of May and attracted an enormous crowd of pilgrims and faithful. Already in the 17th century, however, the

abbey had fallen deeply into decadence; its last abbot, Cardinal Louis of Rohan, was seriously compromised for having made a gift of a precious necklace of enormous value to the Queen Marie Antoinette, which he was not able to pay for. He was tried and, although found innocent, King Louis XVI ordered the suppression of the abbey as punishment in 1786. The abbey was sold several years later to a woman for 62,000 francs, payable over 12 years, but, due to the bankruptcy of the buyer, it was offered to a merchant for a much lower figure (23,000 francs). The latter sold off several parts of the abbey to small property owners who lived there. Finally in the last century the building was recovered and patiently restored. All that remains today of the enormous abbey complex is the **Church of Notre Dame** which stands in splendid isolation on a rocky outcrop; it dates from the 12th century. The crypt is partially carved out of the rock and its cloister, from the end of the same century, is regarded as the finest Romanesque cloister in Provence, after that of St. Trophime in Arles. The capitals offer a superb example of a sculpted bestiary: there is the legendary monster of the «Tarasque,» the Salamander, Jonah and the whale, a knight attacked by a lion.

The *Chapelle St. Pierre* still survives; it was dug out of the rock of the hill, and also the *Chapelle de la Ste. Croix,* a small lovely proportioned building in the form of a Greek cross. The tombs of the monks are also very picturesque. They are shown during their good works; carved out of the stone each has a small cushion of stone supporting the head of the dead man.

*Two views of the Moulin de Daudet.*

## MOULIN DE DAUDET

When Alphonse Daudet, the great writer, born in Nîmes in 1840 and who died in Paris in 1897, came to Fontvieille he stayed with some friends in the castle of Montauban. What is more, he owned a wind-mill. This is the genuine, the actual «windmill of Daudet,» from which the author wrote his «Lettres de mon moulin.» More precisely, from where he imagined writing them, because in fact the letters were written in Paris in 1865 and published four years later. One ar-rives at the windmill, whose mech-anism in still in working order, along a very lovely pine-shaded avenue. Here the Provençal writer, who very finely and delicately de-scribed his land, loved to walk, to wander, to chat with the miller. The mill was restored in 1938 and was later made into a museum which contains mementoes and personal effects of Alphonse Daudet.

*Les Baux-de-Provence - The walls of the ancient castle fuse with the bare rock.*

# LES BAUX-DE-PROVENCE

A barren rocky spur, 900 metres long: here, at a height of 280 metres, there are the remains of a medieval city, with a **castle** in ruins and gutted houses. This is Les Baux today. It was once the seat of a civilized court and the centre of Troubadour poetry. Its impact is truly incredible.

The human habitation of this site goes back to pre-historic times, certainly to the Iron Age, but it is during the Middle Ages that the historical and artistic importance of Les Baux leapt to the fore.

By the end of the 10th century a powerful feudal family had already firmly established itself here and controlled the whole surrounding area. By the end of the following century it was to be one of the strongest families in the whole of southern France, with the control of 79 villages and towns.

«Raco d'eigloun, jamai vassalo» (Race d'aiglons, jamais vassale), that is, «a lineage of eagles, never vassals,» Mistral was to write about its strength and pride. The lords of Les Baux were so proud that they claimed to descend from Balthasar, one of the mythical Magi: to enforce this genealogical claim they added the star-comet with sixteen silver rays to their coat of arms. They were so strong that they were able to vaunt their power at the Counts of Provence from the impregnable rock fortress for several centuries. Theirs is a long and turbulent history of wars and betrayals, of blood and of death. It is not for this, however, that the fame of Les Baux spread quickly throughout feudal Europe. Together with these warrior-princes lived the Troubadours, the new poets who had emerged from feudal society. Here, the most famous Troubadours of the age found protection and shelter: Raimbaut de Vacqueiras, Boniface de Castellane, Guy de Cavaillon. The most famous and seductive of the Provençal «cours d'amour» was held at the court of Les Baux: in the presence of the always noble and gracious lady, love was sung in its highest and most ennobled form. The longing of the troubadour, always unsatisfied and never exhausted, is at the centre of the whole of this new conception of poetry and love. They were concerned with problems of gallantry, of courtship and of chivalry; they played, they danced, they enjoyed themselves, and when there was a winner, he received a crown of peacock's feathers and a kiss from the most beautiful lady.

But finally, even this world had to come to an end. It ended when Alix, the last princess of the Baux lineage, died. Les Baux was taken over by the Counts of Provence and became a simple barony, still later it became a part of the kingdom of France.

In 1528 it enjoyed a brief period of prosperity under

the Constable Anne de Montmorency, and it then became a dangerous focal point of Protestantism. In 1632, Louis XIII, worried by the existence of this restless and turbulent stronghold, decided to have everything demolished, both the castle and the walls.

The small **Church of St. Vincent** still presents us with an elegant 16th century bell-tower called the «lantern of the dead.» It is round in shape and has four arcades, topped by a small dome. It is said that, during the Middle Ages, on the nights when an important citizen died, a flame was lit there. The church still retains and perpetuates a very charming and moving ceremony

*A typical Provençal shop located in an old building; a corner of Jean de Brion's town house; the church of St. Vincent and the 16th century Maison des Porcelets.*

*Another view of the fine dwellings that flank the streets of Les Baux and the fine cross windows of the Hôtel de Manville.*

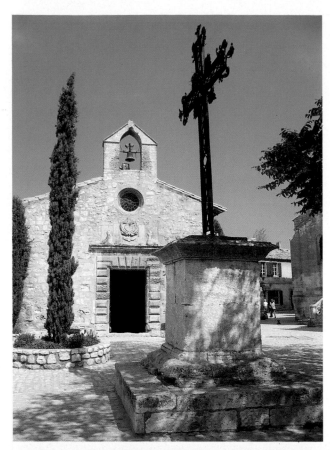

The 17th century chapel known as of the Pénitents Blancs, on Place Saint-Vincents; a 16th century chapel where the Museum of the Provençal «Santons» is now housed; the exterior of the church of St. Blasius, of the 12th century.

An imposing limestone rock eroded by the wind; a view of the «columbarium» and two pictures which reveal what is left of a chapel inside the castle.

*The ruins of the castle and the monument to the poet Charloun Rieu.*

which takes place on Christmas Eve: the *shepherds' mass*. The ceremony goes back to the 16th century and relives the birth of Christ through songs and scenes of a medieval atmosphere. The lamb, which will be offered to the newborn Christ, is placed on a carpet of red wool in a small cart; before it go angels and drummers and behind it come the shepherds with their flocks as it is carried in procession to the high altar of the church. Around the altar a highly symbolic ceremony takes place with dialogue and songs between the angels and the shepherds who bring baskets of fruit and gifts in adoration. At the moment of the elevation of the Host, it is customary to squeeze the lamb's tail hard, three times, to make it bleat at the renewal of Christ's birth.

Near the church is the **Maison des Porcelets**, dating from the 16th century. The ground floor is a huge hall with an ogival vault. There are frescoes from the 17th century, depicting allegorically the four seasons. Another picturesque house is the **Hôtel de Manville**, with a beautiful façade. It was built in 1571 and today houses a Museum of Modern Art. It is impossible to be unmoved by the superb *cross window* in front of the Hôtel, a lonely witness to the destruction of the city. A

The powerful walls of Les Baux seem to emerge from the rock as if by magic.

meaningful inscription beneath the eaves (*Post tenebras, lux*) almost alludes to a new life that unfortunately was not to be for the city and its inhabitants.

There is a magnificent view of the whole complex of Les Baux if we climb up what was once the awe-inspiring castle. Here one side of the rock contains a great number of identical square holes; according to some these contained the cremated ashes of the dead (*columbarium*), or else it is an ancient dovecote. Below, at the foot of the escarpment, the small octagonal temple, the **Pavillon de la reine Jeanne**, from the 16th century, may be seen. It is so lovely that Mistral had a copy of it done for his tomb in Maillane. Mistral was the most famous poet of these places but not the only one: Charloun Rieu, who was born in 1846 and died in 1924, was a peasant-poet, a bard, in love with his land. His admirers wanted to dedicate a **monument** to him and erected it on one of the most beautiful spots of Les Baux. From here the eye can sweep over Arles and the Camargue and, on exceptionally clear days, see as far as Saintes-Maries-de-la-Mer and Aigues-Mortes. Also, we should not forget that this place gave its name to bauxite, the mineral which was discovered here in great quantities in 1822.

*Saint-Rémy-de-Provence - Les Antiques: the Arch and the Cenotaph and a detail of the latter, with the base decorated with mythological scenes in relief.*

# SAINT-RÉMY-DE-PROVENCE

The town of Saint-Rémy-de-Provence was known, until 1921, above all as being the birth-place, in 1503, of Michel de Nostredame; this event took place in a small house in Rue Hoche, he was to become famous for his prophesies and was known by the name Nostradamus.

Then, suddenly, in 1921, archeological excavations unearthed the existence of a city, Glanum, which must have had a good 5,000 inhabitants.

The place which is known today as **Les Antiques** once marked the entrance to the ancient Glanum, and it was inseparable from the latter. The two monuments today that dominate the sun-baked country-side are rather astonishing. The **Cenotaph**, despite the fact that it dates from the 1st century A.D., looks as if it had just emerged from the hands of its architect. It has miraculously escaped both the damage of man and of time and is one of the loveliest monuments of the Roman world, and without doubt the best preserved. It was mistakenly believed for a long time that it was a tomb; it is in fact a mausoleum dedicated to the two nephews of Augustus, Caius and Lucius, who both died very young in battle. The Maison Carrée in Nîmes is also

dedicated to them. It is 19.3 metres high and is made up of a base, decorated with reliefs of mythological stories: the battle of the Amazons, the death of Adonis, the struggle between the Greeks and the Trojans over the body of Patroclus. A first floor has four arches; the second floor is made up of a small circular temple whose Corinthian columns enclose the statues of Caius and Lucius, wrapped in Roman togas. Only the pinecone which should crown the monument is missing for the mausoleum to be absolutely intact. By comparison the **Arch** through which the road from the Alps passed on its way to Milan, is much deteriorated, though of equal importance and fascination. It is the oldest arch in the whole of Narbonian Gaul and is characterized by its precise proportions and the quality of the sculpture that decorates it which shows a certain Greek influence. It has a single arch and is 7.50 metres high; as well as the extremely finely carved garlands of fruit and leaves it is embellished with sculpted groups of prisoners chained to a tree.

Nearby, in a fertile plain where olives and grain are grown, in the vicinity of the Alpilles, the last chain of the Alps, is the ancient **monastery of St.-Paul-de-**

*The landscape around the Alpilles.*

*Saint-Rémy-de-Provence - the Monastery of St.-Paul-de-Mausole.*

**Mausole**, from the end of the 12th century. The founding of this monastery was marked by a miraculous event: a holy man named Paul was offered the bishopric on behalf of the people of Rheims who, having fled the barbarian hordes, had arrived here. The saint replied that he would accept only if when he stuck his staff in the ground it would become covered with flowers. This he did and the event immediately took place. The monastery was then built which today contains the church and the delightful cloister.

At the beginning of the 19th century the Augustinian monastery was made into a rest home and was enlarged: to the sides of the old building two very long and low wings were added which surround the house. The whole complex is immersed in the greenery, among fields and gardens. Here, in May of 1889, Vincent van Gogh came voluntarily to be treated, as may be seen in the register, for «acute mania, accompanied by visual and auditory hallucinations...» During this tragic stay the great artist painted many pictures: some were done in the garden, of flowers, plants and butterflies. There are also the famous cypresses and some portraits, amongst which is the *Self Portrait with palette* done in the garden of the asylum in September 1889, in which the crazed stare of the Dutch painter reveals the inner force which only his tragic and certain death could extinguish.

*Glanum - A view of the excavations and what remains of the so- called «twin temples».*

# GLANUM

Glanum was founded as a sanctuary in the 6th century B.C. by Phoenician merchants around a sacred spring that still fed the pool later built by the Romans. For those travelling from Marseille to Avignon this was an important stopping place, as the large road that came down from the Alps crossed here; in Roman times this would become the via Domitian. This was Glanum with its rich houses, its monumental nymphaeum and its many votive altars dedicated to Hercules, whose worship was ardently practiced here. Following the occupation of Provence by the legions of Marius in 102 B.C., the city sanctuary became Glanum and followed at the same rate the phases of Romanisation of the rest of the province. The excavations at Glanum, since 1921, have brought to light the foundations of three pe-

*The reconstruction of the city of Glanum in a painting
by Pierre Poulain, in the Museum.*

*Plan of the archeological complex of Glanum.*

riods, very different one from the other: the first is
Hellenistic, with remains of houses, nymphaea, temples and baths; the second is Roman; the third to be discovered belonged to the period that went from the occupation of Marseilles in 49 B.C. to the sack of the
city in 270 A.D. The city had already been destroyed
once by the Teutons at the time when they came into
conflict with Marius, it was quickly reconstructed;
then the arrival of the Franks and the Alemans, as sudden as it was brutal, dealt the final blow to the city.

There was, it is true, a moment of recovery and development during the Carolingian period, when the *Villa
of the Saint Rémy* was founded, which then became
St. Rémy. With reference to this there is a Provençal
legend which tells how in the 6th century the Bishop
of Rheims, Rémy, came to Glanum together with
Clovis and tried to exorcise a young woman who was
possessed by the devil. The girl however did not re-
spond to the exorcism and she died. Rémy then brought her back to life and the girl's father, struck by the

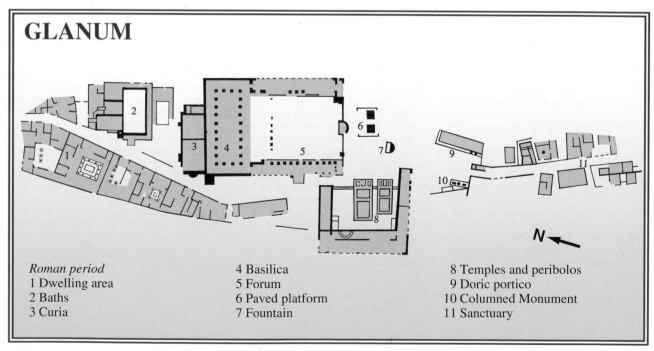

# GLANUM

*Roman period*
1 Dwelling area
2 Baths
3 Curia

4 Basilica
5 Forum
6 Paved platform
7 Fountain

8 Temples and peribolos
9 Doric portico
10 Columned Monument
11 Sanctuary

*A view of the House of the Doors: archeologists gave it this name in view of the two massive fluted piers that frame a room in the house.*

*The reconstruction, dating to 1992, of part of one of the «twin temples».*

miracle, offered the bishop an enormous grant of land which also included a part of Glanum.

The city was then partially covered by the alluvial deposits that came down from the Alpilles. The first diggings, done purely by chance and haphazardly go back to the 18th century when a funerary monument from the 3rd century, dedicated to one Aebutius Agathon, the keeper of the city's treasure at Glanum, was discovered. Later a silver coin was found which bore an engraving of a bull on one side and of the goddess of fertility, Demeter, on the other. This second discovery eliminated the final uncertainties–there was no longer any doubt that there below was a city. And what a city! The **Baths** came to light, whose pools had been sup-

*A corner of the Forum and the Via del Santuario.*

*Two of the buildings in the area of the Sanctuary: the columned monument and the temple of Valetudo.*

*The fine head of a river god found in the pool of the Baths of Glanum and now on exhibit in the Hôtel de Sade, a fine private dwelling of the 16th century in Saint-Rémy-de-Provence where many of the archeological finds from the excavations of Glanum are now kept.*

plied directly from the ancient, sacred spring; then, between a swimming pool and a street an **unctorium** was discovered. This was none other than the equivalent of a modern beauty parlour where massages and beauty treatments for the body were given. The diggings here came across the oldest mosaics in Gaul, depicting four dolphins. There was also a covered canal, perhaps the remains of the ancient system of drains whose covering formed the paving of Glanum's main street. At the limits of Glanum, next to the very ancient Sanctuary, is the **Nymphaeum**, built on the site where the spring which gave the city its origin was found; it was restored in 20 A.D. by Agrippa. Here, water which was able to cure all ills, coming from the mountain, gushed forth: for this the Romans venerated Apollo, the god of healing. There were also many altars dedicated to Hercules who is represented in many different attitudes in the statuary: the *Hercules Bibax*, the *Hercules Victor*...

*Panorama overlooking the Rhône and the city.*

# TARASCON

Tarascon was established as a commercial colony of Marseille at first on an island in the middle of the Rhône: it was called Jovarnica or Gernica. The island was joined to to the left bank of the river by alluvial deposits, and in time a Roman camp was founded here, called Tarusco. Perhaps it was the troubled appearance of the river that gave birth to the legend which made Tarascon famous. In a very old literary source, the hagiography of St. Martha, the story of the Tarasque is mentioned for the first time; this was a monster, half animal and half-fish, which lived hidden in the woods along the banks of the river. When it emerged it killed anything that passed by, be it man or beast. It seems the monster was called Tirascurus because it hid in a place known as Nerluc, that is, the sacred black wood. All attempts against it were in vain; one day when it was surprised by sixteen youths, it ate eight of them. It was at that time that St. Martha arrived here from Saintes-Maries-de-la-Mer, preaching the Christian gospel in these parts. The saint drew close to the mon-

ster, bathed it in holy water and showed it a wooden cross; the terrifying beast became tame. Then the woman bound her girdle around its neck and led it to the locals who killed it with stones and blows from a lance.

The Tarasque legend has come down to us in many forms: sculpted in stone, in wood, or painted, on the church doors and on the streets corners, or remembered in simple folk representations. However another very lively and unique form survives in Tarascon: that of the local holiday and of the procession. The 14th April 1474 is the date on which the famous «roi René» founded the order of the Knights of the Tarasque: the celebrations that followed it were highly symbolic and included games with a representation of the animal and holy processions in honour of St. Martha; this took place on no precise day of the year, perhaps Ascension or Pentecost. Nowadays the last Sunday in June and the 29th July (the feast of St. Martha) see the monster still carried through the city in the form of an enor-

*General view of the Castle.*

mous paper-maché dragon whose head and tail are moved by eight young people from the inside, symbolizing the eight boys eaten by the monster. The city's name is also associated with the adventures of Tartarin (which are in fact comic but which his incredible imagination makes extraordinary), the central character of three famous novels by Daudet: *Aventures véritables de Tartarin de Tarascon,* 1872; *Tartarin sur les Alpes,* 1885; *Port-Tarascon,* 1890. Whether he goes to Africa to kill a lion, tries to climb the Alps, or leaves for Australia to found a colony, Tartarin is fascinating for the lies, the bragging and the incredible stories of which he is the protagonist.

St. Martha and the terrible dragon, Daudet and the enjoyable Tartarin are two traditions which are rooted and now inseparable in Tarascon. The city possesses other, and very visible, beauties too. The most important of all is the famous **Castle**, among the most beautiful in France and without doubt the most beautiful in Provence as an example of feudal Gothic architecture.

This castle was built on the remains of a Roman camp as the royal residence of the Anjou-Provençal dynasty; it aggressively faces the castle of Beaucaire, on the opposite bank of the Rhône. The severe military and feudal appearance of the exterior contrasts with the elegance and grace of the interior which already anticipates the Renaissance. Its period of greatest splendour was under the «bon roi René» who, dividing his time between the castle at Aix and this one, decided that this was his favourite residence. From the 16th century on it was reduced to being a prison: in 1794, during the Revolution many of Robespierre's partisans met a horrible death here (they were thrown from the height of the walls into the river). The castle relinquished this sad role only in 1926 when it was restored and opened to the public; it assumed once again the appearance it must have had five centuries ago, surrounded by a moat in whose water the warm colour of the stone is reflected. The castle is made up of two parts: the lower, enclosed by walls and reinforced at the corners

with rectangular towers; the other, the palace itself with round corner towers.

The **courtyard**, in Flemish-Gothic style, is a little masterpiece of grace and elegance. It has a polygonal spiral staircase with rich carving at the base and, on high, in a niche, are *the busts of King René and Queen Joan de Laval.* There is a loggia, too perfect and delicate, for us not to recognize the hand of Francesco Laurana. The interior also reveals a taste that is no longer feudal. Large fire-places and pretty windows open and beautify the walls of the hall, the same walls, which at one time must have rung with the festive echoes of the happy court life under the «bon roi René.» The life of the prisoners,

*The back of the castle and the gallery flanking the court of honour.*

*Two pictures of the court of the Castle with the busts of King René and Queen Joan de Laval.*

*General view of the collegiate church of Ste.-Marthe.*

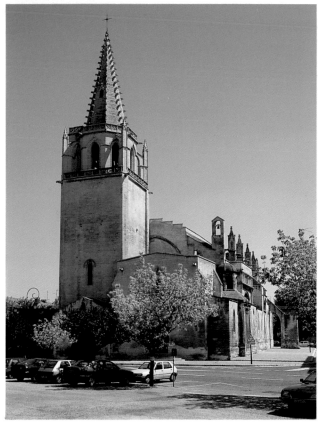

however, walled up in the Tour de l'Horloge must have been much less happy; particularly for those who wiled away the interminable hours of solitude by scratching and carving laments and drawings on the walls. Who knows what meaning that engraved boat must have had, almost a desperate memory of a freedom now lost.

Almost directly in front of the castle is the **Church of Ste.-Marthe** whose existence was documented already in the 10th century but which became important only from 1187, when the body of the saint was rediscovered. The church, which was consecrated ten years later, was for the most part rebuilt during the 14th century. The interior, with a nave, two aisles and composite pillars, contains the double tomb of St. Martha in the crypt. One, from the 16th century, shows the saint on a sarcophagus decorated with pillars and bas reliefs; the other, in Baroque style, encloses the early tomb, a Christian coffin from the 5th century.

Nearby is the rue des Halles whose picturesque 15th century arcaded houses evoke a whole world that has now disappeared; at the beginning of the street is the 17th century **Hôtel de Ville.**

*What remains of the castle which once dominated Beaucaire.*

*View from the top of the abbey of Saint-Michel-de-Frigolet and the sumptuous interior of the chapel of Notre-Dame-du-Bon-Remède.*

# BEAUCAIRE

Beaucaire was built over the site of the Roman Ugernum and was then the Merovingian capital of Pagus Argenteus, and the twin city of Tarascon. For seven centuries the two castles menacingly faced each other, and for the whole of the Middle Ages there was a continuous race for fortification, foreseeing an attack that was never to come.

The **Castle**, characterized by a beautiful tower on a triangular base (a rare phenomenon), was destroyed by order of Richelieu in 1632.

But what brought Beaucaire to fame, a fame which lasted from the 13th to the last century, was a fair, which today, unfortunately, no longer exists.

It was instituted in 1217 by Raymond VI, Count of Toulouse and the city immediately became the French market «capital.» Every year, in July, the city changed completely. Those unable to find a place in the hotels lodged in private houses; those without accommodations in private homes made do with sleeping on the boats docked at the port. Each street of the city specialized in a particular ware: some sold only wine and some sold only jewels. Some sold oriental perfumes and others rice from Lombardy; some honey from Narbonne and others corals and strings of pearls. Those in love gave their ladies rings of glass to symbolize the beauty and the fragility of love. Some bought rough silk and others bought weapons; the smell of cocoa mixed with that of cinnamon and the hot aroma of coffee with the bitterness of oranges and lemons; and then again there was delicate porcelain alongside strong draughthorses, very fine lace next to cottons from Rouen.

Even the Marquis de Sade tried his fortune here in 1797, he launched a lottery, but its failure was such that he gave it up immediately. According to tradition the companies of acrobats and jugglers presented their new «numbers» here before beginning their tours of Europe and so alongside the merchants mingled dwarfs, trained dogs, monkeys and bearded women, acrobats and liontamers.

The arrival of the railways unfortunately rudely interrupted the centuries-old Fair of Beaucaire.

# ABBEY OF SAINT-MICHEL-DE-FRIGOLET

The pleasant valley of the Frigolet owes its name to the aromatic thyme which grows here and which the Provençals call «farigoulo». The first official notice of the existence of an abbey dates to 1133 when various nobles make a rich donation of about 50 hectares of land to the church of Saint-Michel, founded - apparently - by the monks of Montmajour who often came here to treat the fevers they had caught in their region. This also led to the building of a chapel dedicated to **Notre-Dame-du-Bon-Remède**, in Provençal Romanesque, and which now constitutes the apse of the 19th century abbey. Anne of Austria, Louis XIII's wife, as thanks to the Virgin for having born a child, had the church decorated with sumptuous gilded boiseries and with the twelve canvasses of the school of Nicolas Mignard which we can still admire today. The history of Père Gaucher is also part of this abbey. He had distilled an elixir of herbs and the alembic in which it was prepared is still to be seen in a room next to the cloister. The liquor, now more simply and easily produced by a Provençal firm, is for sale in the abbey's shop.

# ABBEY OF SAINT-ROMAN

Saint-Roman is an abbey set in caves whose foundation supposedly goes back to the 5th century although there are no supporting documents. There is however no doubt that this rock abbey is one of the oldest monasteries in France and that the site is also particularly lovely and evocative. Defensive works were erected to protect the monastic community which lived in isolation up here in the rocks, and the abbey acquired the aspect of a true fortress. Unfortunately as time passed parts were torn down and the original aspect of the abbey has been completely altered. An excellent itinerary marked by arrows of various colors leads the visitor through the entire monastic complex, beginning with the *chapel* which is actually simply an enormous natural cave which the monks turned into a place of prayer. Here, in the choir part, is the so-called «*tomb of St. Roman*», where it is said a fragment of the saint's right hand is preserved. Passing from the terrace from which a magnificent panorama over the Rhône can be had, and where the monastery cemetery is to be found, one descends to the cells: on the architrave of a door a Latin inscription tells us that the monk Vitalis lived here. Of particular interest is the cistern which had a capacity of up to 140,000 liters of rain water, as is the *great hall* (12 meters high and 17 meters long) which was originally divided into three superposed rooms, all patiently excavated, like the entire abbey, by the hand of man.

# NÎMES

Spread out at the feet of the limestone hills of the Garrigues the city of Nîmes welcomes us with its cheerful and lively appearance. It is a very important wine-making centre and its development over recent years is due to the rich beds of coal that have given rise to a number of industries, above all metallurgical, chemical and textile (especially silk). Nîmes was so indelibly marked by Roman civilization that, because of the monuments and remains of that period, it gained the title «the French Rome.»

But even before the Romans arrived this place was already inhabited by an early historical settlement: tombs and fragments of terracotta and statues found during excavations are a testimony of this. The ancient name for Nîmes was Nemausus, it was a sanctuary that grew up alongside a spring used by the local population who worshipped a god of the same name, and which continued to be venerated even by the Romans. The city became the capital of the Volcae Areconae tribe and was quickly occupied by the Romans, more precisely the veterans of Octavian (who was to become Augustus), who had defeated Antony and Cleopatra in Egypt.

This is why, still today, on the coat of arms of the city there is a representation of a chained crocodile, the symbol of the conquest of Egypt, in gratitude for which this lovely Provençal city was given to Octavian's veterans. Nîmes lived its golden age under Roman dominion, it was enlarged, fortified and enriched with monuments; under the Antonines it replaced Narbonne as capital of Gallia Narbonense.

At the end of the period of Roman conquest the sad and ominous times of religious struggle began. From the 5th century onwards they were characterized by the spread and persecution of the Arian heresy which came to an end only in the 8th century. In the 13th century Nîmes became the centre of the Albigensian heresy until 1226 when it was conquered by Louis VIII. Also due to the arrival of efficient Italian artisans Nîmes became a flourishing centre for the textile industry; its velvets and cloth of gold became very famous.

The wars of religion, however, continued for a long time to upset the city: in 1389 the Jews were exiled; since the 7th century they had enjoyed comparative peace and relative prosperity. In the 16th century Nîmes became Calvinist and the factions which were tearing apart the country also afflicted this tranquil Provençal city. Unhappily famous in its history is the

*Three pictures of the rock-cut abbey of Saint-Roman: a view of the chapel, the bishop's throne and the necropolis on the terrace.*

*A view of the arena and, in the foreground, ruins of Roman date.*

*The interior of the amphitheatre.*

day, commemorated by the name Michelade, St. Michael's day, the 27th September 1576, when the Catholics were massacred. The Revocation of the Edict of Nantes in 1685 which had been promulgated to clarify the position of the Calvinists destroyed the prosperity which, despite its internal strife, the city had enjoyed up to that time. The French Revolution calmed the animosity up to a certain point, but then in 1815 a long series of violent outbreaks and murders took place, the so-called «White Terror,» the work of the bandits Trestaillons and Truphemy, incited by the extremist nobility.

In more recent times Nîmes has expanded beyond its circle of walls and has experienced a development that has not yet stopped. But now let us go back in time to appreciate the monuments of this «French Rome.»

To say Nîmes is to say the **Arena**, the amphitheatre where gladiatorial fights and struggles against wild beasts took place. Of all the Roman amphitheatres that have come down to us, from the point of view of size this one only takes the twentieth place, but it is amongst the finest for its excellent state of preservation. It was built in the second half of the 1st century A.D. and has a perfect elliptical form with two orders of Doric columns crowned by an upper level in which were the brackets for the stakes of the velarium. It measures 133 metres by 101 metres and 24,000 spectators were able to be seated on 34 levels of steps, which

were subdivided according to different social classes (there were also places reserved for particular people). Each step was divided into 40-centimetre sections which were the spaces alotted to each spectator. The layout of the entrance galleries was made in such a way that the spectator had easy access to each level of steps. Not only this but there also existed a small stairway that enabled the men whose job was to set up the velarium to get up to the upper level without disturbing the spectators: none other, in fact, than our modern service stairs. The amphitheatre was used for a long time, until the 5th century when the Visigoths turned it into a fortress, having also dug a defensive moat around the building. In the Middle Ages it became a place of refuge and safety for the poor who built small houses and a chapel there. During the last century it was finally restored and put back into use. From 1863 onwards the corridas began to be held here which were always watched, then as now, by a crowd which filled to overflowing the steps of the Arena.

The lack of decoration may surprise us but it is the very particular kind of material used in its construction that is hard to carve. Some examples do remain however, *a fight between gladiators,* and another, on a pillar on the ground floor, is a *bas relief of the Capitoline she-wolf suckling Romulus and Remus.*

The other symbol of Nîmes is the **Maison Carrée**, the Roman temple from which Napoleon Bonaparte drew

*The elegant simplicity of the Maison Carrée.*

inspiration for the construction of the Madeleine. Built during the reign of Augustus, perhaps by Agrippa to honour the memory of the two sons he had by Julia, the daughter of Augustus, both of whom died very young. Built in the 1st century B.C., it has come down to us in an almost perfect state of preservation, despite the troubled events to which its history is linked. It also later became the city hall and a church for the Augustine order, Fortunately it escaped the fate planned for it by Colbert which was to dismantle it completely and rebuild it, exactly as it was, at Versailles. Since the 16th century it has been called the Maison Carrée, even though it is not exactly square; it is 26 metres long, 15 wide and 17 high. It is not, therefore, very large in scale but it is very elegant and harmonious in the thrust of the 30 fluted Corinthian columns that support the architrave around which runs a very finely-made frieze, surmounted by the tympanum. Inside, a small **Museum of Antiquity** has been laid out; there are archeological finds from the Imperial age.

Exceptional among the many pieces found during the excavations are a beautiful *head of Apollo* in bronze, an enormous *statue of Apollo,* found in the ruins of the Baths of the Fountain, many mosaics, and a *statue of Venus* which was discovered burnt, was restored, and is called the Nîmes Venus.

Other important discoveries are not here but in the Archeological Museum which is one of the most important in France, particularly for the sculpture section: one exhibit shows the *head of a Gallic warrior,* tremendous and terrifying in an enormous stylized helmet that covers the whole head; another with soft lines, represents the *head of Jupiter Serapis.*

The **Tour Magne** is another curiosity of Nîmes, also because it is linked to a strange story of a «gold hunter.» The Turris Magna, on the top of Mont Cavalier, was originally a part of the city's circle of walls: in fact it was probably the most important part. It was put up at the end of the 1st century B.C. and stands on an octagonal base; the lower part has deep niches, on top of which there is a floor without decoration and finally an upper level with Tuscan pillars. This is all that is left, but originally the tower must have had yet another floor with half-columns. The tower, which is presently 30 metres high, has in fact, during the centuries, lost almost 10 metres in height. Its use remains unknown, whether it was a tomb, a trophy, a watchtower, who knows? It is certain however that it is strangely reminiscent of the famous lighthouse of Alexandria which was built in 280 B.C. Its history, as we have said is linked to that of a certain François Traucat, a gardener, who in 1601, having read in the Prophecies of Nostradamus that a gardener would become rich and famous by the discovery of hidden treasure, took it into his head that the treasure

was close at hand, buried under the walls of the Tour Magne; there he began to dig.

Inevitably there was no trace of the treasure, but unwittingly he discovered something else, which was that the walls of the Roman period were raised on a dry stone tower from Gallic times whose existence, until that time, no-one had ever suspected.

Like all Roman colonies Nîmes also had its complex of baths. Here, however, it was closely linked to the spring dedicated to the god Nemausus, whose temple has disappeared; this water fed the baths which were erected in the 2nd century. In Roman times the enormous complex included a theatre and a temple as well as the spring and the baths. Today there remain only the ruins of the baths, otherwise known as the **Temple of Diana** but which, in reality, is not a temple in the true sense, nor connected with the goddess whose name it bears. In fact, it seems probable that this building was used to lodge the believers in the god Nemausus, but these are only suppositions. The roofing system is interesting as it uses opposing arches to support the vault. The **Fountain Garden**, on the other hand, is the product of the military engineering of the 18th century. The spring is here and it was constructed with geometrically arranged basins on different levels surrounded by a balustrade. The pool and the double flight of stairs that led to the spring are still visible today. By comparison with this complex and magnificent building the «**castellum divisorium**» may appear modest; this is the water castle, the point of arrival of the Nîmes aqueduct, dating from Roman times. Though modest it is of great technical interest, because buildings of this kind that have survived from the ancient world are very rare. It was built in 19 B.C. on the side of a hill to the north of the city and discovered in 1844; it is circular in form and is surrounded by elevated pavements. Its purpose was to bring water from a spring near Uzès to Nîmes, as the water from the local spring was insufficient for the whole city. But, due to the considerable technical difficulties caused by a slight difference in height of the canal's point of departure and its point of arrival, the Romans hoped to supply the city by making the water pass through a new distribution basin. This was controlled by a lock that distributed the water in five different directions and from here to the whole city. It is estimated that this basin supplied at least 20,000 cubic metres of water a day, that is approximately 400 litres for each of the 50,000 inhabitants of Nemausus.

Unfortunately the **Porte d'Arles** is for the most part in ruins. It is also called the Gate of Augustus, and was part of the circle of walls built in 15 B.C. It marked the place of arrival of the Via Domitia, which was named in honour of the consul Cneius Domitius Ahenobarbus; the road ran from Beaucaire to Nîmes, here it entered the city and became its natural decumanus maximus (main thoroughfare). The gate had four openings: the two, more important, were in the centre for the passage of vehicles, the outer ones were narrower and were used by pedestrians. In the open space beyond the gate is a *statue of Augustus* which is a copy of the Roman original.

*The imposing mass of the Tour Magne and a detail of the «cella» of the Temple of Diana.*

Two views of the Gate of Augustus, with the bronze statue of the emperor.

Marble vases and statues surround the Nemausus spring inside the 18th century Garden of the Fountain.

# PONT DU GARD

It was Agrippa, the son-in-law of Augustus, who decided in 19 B.C. to construct an enormous aqueduct to supply Nîmes with drinking water. The bridge that we see today, boldly bestriding the river Gard, is the most majestic part of that wonderful work which has remained almost intact for nearly two thousand years.

It was destroyed during the invasions of the 3rd century but was repaired many times; during the last century it was still in use as a pedestrian bridge.

It is a wonderful example, not only from a technical point of view, but also from an aesthetic one, for the delicate colour of the stone and for the elegance and originality of its construction. For this reason many artists, writers, poets and painters have immortalised it.

The architect who planned it used enormous blocks of stone in its construction, blocks of a good six tons which were raised to a height of 49 metres and secured without the use of cement. The novelty of the bridge is that it is made up of three levels of receding arches placed one above the other and, therefore, completely independent of each other. The measurements of each series of arches are different from those of the others and in this way the entire architectural mass seems invested with its own life. The total height of the bridge from the water level of the river is 40 metres, the first series of six arches has a total length of 142 metres, the central arcade, made up of 11 arches is 242 metres long and the upper level, the third, has 35 arches and is 275 metres long.

*A fascinating view of the Pont du Gard.*

*Panorama of the city, with the Bishop's palace and the Tour Fenestrelle in the background.*

# UZÈS

The most striking thing at Uzès is its typically medieval appearance. The Uzès dynasty is very ancient, the female branch of the house goes back in fact to Charlemagne but only in 1565 did a descendant receive the title of Duke of Uzès from Charles IX.
Life in the village was peaceful for several centuries. Only in 1560, when the Reformation began to be preached in Uzès also, did things began to change. The war of religion tore apart the village for a long time as the villagers divided themselves into Catholics and Protestants.
In 1661 Jean Racine, hardly 22 years old, arrived in Uzès. He had been sent there by his family who witnessed with anxiety the powerful fascination that the theatre exerted over the young man, to stay with an uncle who was the vicar general of the village. He had just left a strict Jansenist college in Paris. Racine stayed with his uncle for less than a year but the letters that he wrote to his family are little concerned with theological problems and mainly concerned with poetical ones. The beauties of the countryside are remembered more frequently than those of the spirit; and so, when he returned to Paris, he was more convinced than ever of the choice by which he would pass into the history of the theatre and literature.
The town is dominated today, as it was then, by the feudal bulk of the castle, called the **Duché**, which belonged to the dukes of Uzès. It is a strong quadrilateral structure put up between the 13th and 14th centuries. In the courtyard there is a strange contrast between the two towers (the Tour de la Vicomté of the 14th century and the Tour Bermonde of the 11th) and the Renaissance façade that stands on the left. It was built in 1550 from a design by Philibert Delorme who conceived of the three orders, the Doric, the Ionic and the Corinthian, placed one above the other: what we find

here at Uzès is one of the first examples of this kind of architectural solution.

Truly unique in the whole of France is the **Tour Fenestrelle** that stands to the right of the cathedral of St. Théodorit. This is all that is left of the early Romanesque cathedral that was destroyed during the furor of the wars of religion. It is 42 metres high and stands on a square foundation though it is round; it has six levels of circular openings each narrower than the one below, and each with openings of a different size. This gives the whole architectural ensemble a certain elegance, lightness of style and variety.

*The entrance to the «Duché» of Uzès.*

*The façade of the cathedral and the Tour Fenestrelle.*

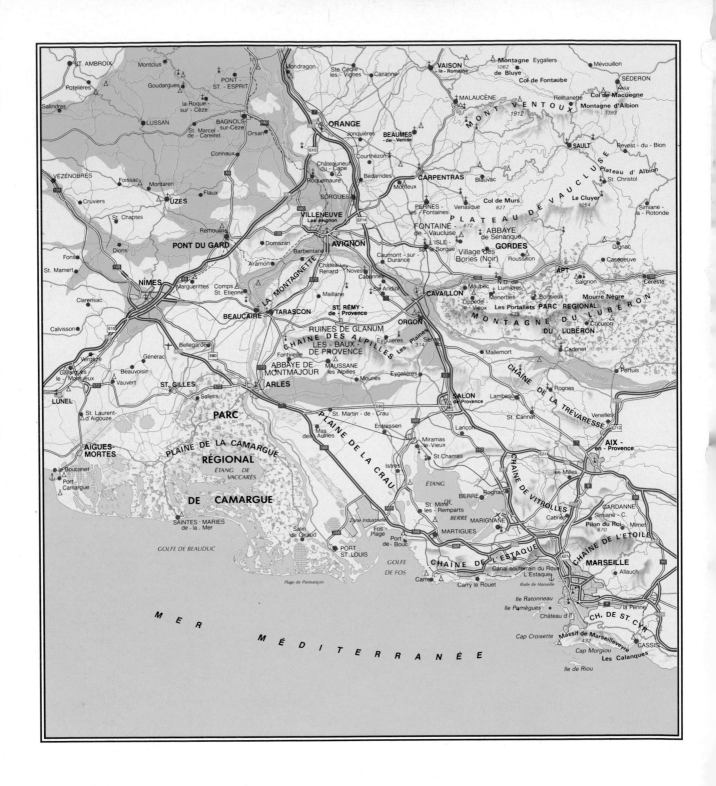